Religions
of the
World

The Editors of Larousse

PETER BEDRICK BOOKS

NTC/Contemporary Publishing Group

**Library of Congress
Cataloging-in-Publication Data**
is available from the
United States Library of Congress.

This volume forms part of the Young
People's Encyclopaedia. It was
produced under the editorial direction
of Claude Naudin and Marie-Lise Cuq.
Text contributors: Michèle Jarton,
Dominique Joly, Colette Kessler, and
Anne-Marie Lelorrain, assisted by
Olivier Cornu and Anne Luthaud.

Graphic design and art direction by
Anne Boyer, assisted by
Emmanuel Chaspoul
Technical coordination by
Pierre Taillemite
Layout by Claudine Combalier
Proofreading, revision by Annick
Valade, assisted by Isabelle Dupré,
Françoise Moulard, and Édith Zha
Picture editing by Anne-Marie
Moyse-Jaubert
Picture research by Michèle Kernéïs
Production by Annie Botrel
Page makeup by Palimpseste
Cover by Gérard Fritsch, assisted by
Véronique Laporte

The editor would like to thank
Dr. Raïs, director of cultural affairs of
the Mosquée de Paris, for his advice.

Original title:
Les Religions du Monde

English translation by
Donald Gecewicz

First published in the United States in
2000 by Peter Bedrick Books
A division of NTC/Contemporary
Publishing Group, Inc.
4255 West Touhy Avenue
Lincolnwood (Chicago), Illinois
60712-1975 U.S.A.
Copyright © 1995 by Larousse-Bordas
Translation copyright © 2000 by
NTC/Contemporary Publishing
Group, Inc.
Printed in France
International Standard Book Number:
0-87226-604-4

00 01 02 03   8 7 6 5 4 3 2 1

Religions of the World

From ancient times to today, throughout the world, the different religions have always been part of Man's life.

how to use this book

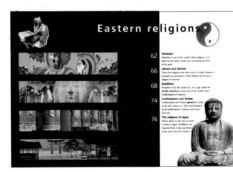

This volume is divided into three sections. Every section is introduced by a contents list that sets out the various chapters and gives a short summary of each.
Special picture-spreads are included between the chapters to reproduce superb images illustrating scenes of religious life in ancient times and today.
The closing pages contain dates, important or little-known facts, a chart of world religions, and a list of the principal deities.
Finally, an index helps you to find quickly the page containing the information you are looking for.

LIVING

x Young People's Encyclopedia

chapter title
Each chapter unfolds over either one or two spreads.

introductory text
This summarizes the broad outline of the subject to be described in the chapter.

panoramic photograph
This illustrates one of the topics of the chapter.

margins
These contain information on additional subjects.

Shinto and Buddhism are the two main religions of Japan. Shinto began in Japan, while Buddhism arrived there in the 6th century and developed in unique ways.

The religions of Japan

A Shintoist purification beneath a waterfall

◀ altar: table or surface on which offerings to deities are placed or sacrifices are made.
◀ amulet: an object meant to protect from evil the person who wears it or keeps it near.
◀ bodhisattva: a sage who takes a vow to save all beings and to help those who suffer instead of achieving nirvana.
◀ cult: worship rendered to a god or a deity; ceremony in which that worship is rendered.
◀ enlightenment: condition of reaching total understanding of the human soul and of the world.
◀ kami: a deity of Shinto. The kami are invisible and cannot be represented. The most important kami is the sun goddess, Amaterasu, whose name means "she who illuminates the sky."
◀ martial arts: a group of combat sports of Japanese origin, including judo, karate, and aikido.
◀ shrine: building consecrated to religious ceremonies; holy place.
◀ torii: a large gate that stands in the sacred area in front of the entrance to Shinto temples.

The oldest religion of Japan is Shinto, which combines the cult of the ancestors with veneration of nature. Its deities are spirits or **kami**. In the 6th century, Buddhism spread into the upper classes of Japanese society. The emperors continued to practice Shintoist rites, however, to avoid offending the people, who mainly remained loyal to the traditional beliefs. In the 19th century, Shinto was proclaimed the national religion. Nowadays, the Japanese mix practices from both religions.

Shintoism
The word "Shinto" means "way of the kami." Originally the kami were the souls of dead ancestors who took shelter in such natural places as waterfalls, ocean waves, or volcano craters. Later, they came to signify those elements possessing extraordinary energy such as the sun, the moon, the trees, or the wind. They can be benevolent or malevolent.

Legends, first written down in the 8th century, recount the creation of the world and the birth of the kami and of Japan. The kami use messengers: the fox is the messenger of Inari, who protects men from evil and brings riches. The kami are consulted at

The fox, messenger of the kami Inari

every opportunity, such as before a journey or an examination, to cure a sick person, to curse an enemy, to ward off bad luck, or to have a child.

The Shinto shrine
In Japanese homes there is a small **altar** dedicated to the family kami and before which **amulets** are placed. These amulets are usually wooden arrows or strips of paper bearing the name of a famous **shrine**. A shrine is the residence of the kami of a place. The believer who goes to invoke a spirit first crosses the great gateway, the **torii**, which marks the entrance to the sacred space. Then he purifies himself by rinsing his mouth and washing his hands in a basin or in a natural spring within the shrine. He then goes into the room for worship (*haiden*) but does not enter the principal room (*honden*) because this is the home of the kami. After dropping a coin in the offering box, he rings the bell and claps his hands three times to advise the kami of his presence. Then he bows and recites his prayer.

Pure Land and Zen Buddhism
Arriving from China and Korea, Buddhism spread to Japan at the end of the 6th century and gave rise to various schools derived from the Mahayana branch (the Great Vehicle). The most popular form of Buddhism in Japan is Pure Land Buddhism, venerating the Buddha Amida. It emerged in India and reached Japan in the 10th century. Buddha Amida is the Buddha of infinite light and is honored by repeating phrases such as "Glory to the Buddha Amida."

Zen Buddhism, which flourished from the 12th century, was also imported from China and has had great influence. Its purpose is to achieve enlightenment through intense

meditation and severe physical discipline. Practicing martial arts, contemplating a garden of sand, and meditating for several hours are all methods of Zen. The spirit of Zen manifests itself in the tea ceremony and in the art of flower arranging, known as "ikebana."

Ceremonies, festivals, and pilgrimages
Buddhism and Shinto are closely interwoven. Under the influence of Buddhism, kamis have become the patron gods of temples and are represented with attributes of bodhisattvas. Buddhist monks also participate

Zen monk meditating before a garden of sand

in Shinto festivals. The Japanese marry in Shinto shrines and celebrate funerals in Buddhist monasteries.

To fulfil a vow or to gain salvation for themselves or for someone who has died, the Japanese go on pilgrimages to holy places or shrines where the deities reside. In shrines or before statues they leave messages on which are written their name and their wishes. To invoke the kami of the mountains or that of the village and to ensure its goodwill, the Japanese organize festivals such as the spring and new year festivals. These generally include performances of dancing or sumo wrestling and archery competitions. ▫

Votive offerings to Inari
These are objects or strips of paper (above) left in a shrine by the faithful to thank a god or to make a request.

Position of the hands in Zen meditation
This traditional position taken during meditation is called "Hakkaiyo-in," which signifies the universe.

It is one of the mudras, symbolic gestures of the hands, with special positions of the fingers. Each of these positions has a religious meaning and expresses a particular sentiment.

76

77

mini-dictionary
The difficult words, marked in bold in the text, are defined here.

caption
Photographs and diagrams are always captioned and are in some cases accompanied by longer scientific or technical explanations.

heading
Each subsection expands on a basic aspect of the subject.

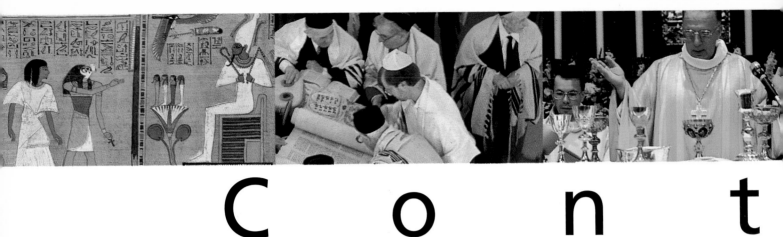

C o n t

e n t s

Since the dawn of humanity, people have believed in something supernatural, above and beyond visible reality. They have tried to explain mysteries like birth, death, the origin of the world . . .

The Religions: beliefs a

- ⦿ **cult:** worship rendered to a god or a deity; ceremony in which that worship is rendered.
- ⦿ **myth:** legendary tale that seeks to explain the origin of humankind or of the world.
- ⦿ **prayer:** a thought directed to God (or to a deity) or the text recited when addressing God (or a deity).
- ⦿ **ritual:** all the religious practices and ceremonies carried out within the framework of a belief or religion.
- ⦿ **superstition:** a belief in mysterious forces, which cannot be explained by reason, and which are regarded as signs that may bring good or bad luck.
- ⦿ **tolerance:** the capacity to accept and respect the beliefs and practices of others.

As far back as Paleolithic (early Stone Age) times, early people buried their dead with weapons, jewelry, and everyday objects as if for use in another life, the life they would live after death. Also from very early times, people seem to have speculated about the origins of life. They wondered what caused phenomena that they could not explain: lightning, thunder, winds, night and day, the cycle of the seasons, and so on. Such events were ascribed to the intervention of one or more all-powerful gods. So it seems that humans have always felt the need to communicate with the gods to maintain their goodwill. The totality of what humankind believes and does in honor of supernatural powers constitutes religion.

The role of religion in society

In all ancient societies, religion played a central role. It was for religious reasons that the first works of art were created, and religion underlay the organization of society and family life and marked the actions of each day. It was unthinkable for someone not to practice a religion, and it was rare for different religions

Buddhist monk at prayer

to exist in the same country without leading to war or persecution. Nowadays, **tolerance** exists in many countries where several religions coexist, and it is accepted that each person may follow the religion of his or her own choosing or follow no religion. However, there are also countries where all laws are based on a single religion and where people with different opinions or beliefs are persecuted.

Beliefs and sacredness, the foundations of religion

Religions are made up of a body of beliefs. Animists believe that in nature there are innumerable invisible spirits. Polytheists believe in several gods, while monotheists believe in only one god. However, many polytheists and animists believe that a principal god is the source of all creation, a point on which they agree with monotheists. In all these types of religion, this deity is beyond the "ordinary" world and is sacred, inspiring profound respect. Believers pass down, by word of mouth and in writing, stories or **myths** concerning their gods, which together form their mythology. Although varied, some of these myths recur in several religions, such as myths of an earthly paradise, of the creation of humankind, and of a great flood. In some religions, believers hold that God communicates directly with people; these are "revealed religions." People who

d practices

a Brahman reading Hindu sacred texts

Roman Catholic religious ceremony

The flood myth

Some religions have points in common. An example is the flood myth, which perhaps conveys people's fear of floods long ago. In the Bible, Noah was the only man to be saved from the flood sent by God to punish humankind for evil-doing. He built a ship, the ark, and took on board two of each animal species (below). It rained for forty days and forty nights, after which Noah's ark came to rest on a mountain. A Mesopotamian myth without doubt inspired the biblical story: the god Ea advises the first man, Uta Napishti, to build a boat to escape the flood. In Greek myth, Zeus sends a flood, but saves Deucalion and Pyrrha, who build an ark.

believe neither in the existence of God nor of any other deity are known as atheists, a name that means "without god." Others think that humankind can know nothing about the origins of the universe or its destiny: these people are referred to as agnostics, signifying that they are indifferent to religious belief.

Religious practices and observances

People who practice a religion and fulfill its commandments are referred to as the faithful. Many among them may affirm that they belong to a religion without, however, doing all that it requires: these people are nonpracticing believers. In every religion, the faithful carry out specific acts that, according to them, are required by their god. **Cult** is the name for all the practices linked to a religion: it includes ceremonies, such as holy festivals marking different stages of life or of the year, and **prayers** of entreaty or thanksgiving. Ceremonies and prayers can be organized according to precise rules or **ritual**. In most religions, designated persons are responsible

for interpreting religious texts and seeing that worship is properly organized. These people, usually priests, constitute the clergy. There are religions without clergy, with no intermediary between an individual and the god (or gods) in which he or she believes. Some believers think that certain, usually secret, words or actions can constrain the forces of nature to do what they want. This is magic—used to obtain a cure, to have good luck, to foretell the future, or to harm an enemy. Those who do not believe in such practices regard magic as **superstition**. ☐

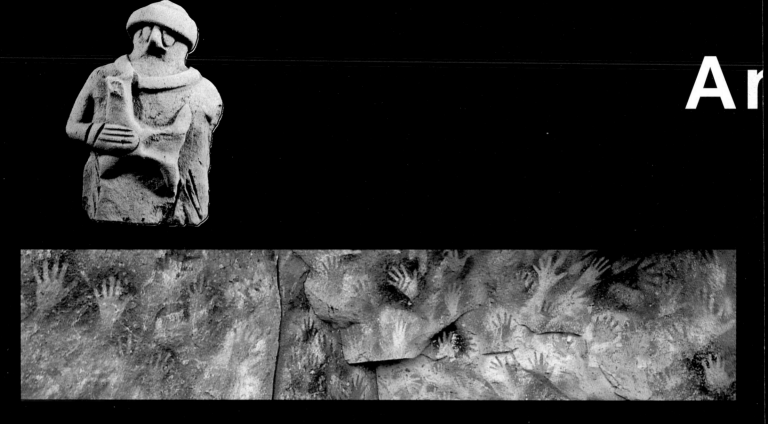

cient Religions

It is difficult to prove that prehistoric people practiced a religion. Archaeological discoveries, however, indicate that the first human societies shared certain beliefs.

The   first beliefs

- **barrow: mound formed of a mass of earth, which was erected above a tomb.**
- **cairn: mass of stones usually covering a dolmen.**
- **cult: worship rendered to a god or a deity; ceremony in which that worship is rendered.**
- **dolmen (from Breton *dol* or *taol*, "table," and *men*, "stone"): prehistoric monument consisting of a horizontal stone slab resting on vertical standing stones.**
- **fertility: quality of being able to reproduce, of being able to have children. In ancient religious beliefs the earth's fertility was compared to a woman's fertility.**
- **grave: place where a dead person is buried.**
- **megalith: prehistoric monument made up of several large blocks of stone. The main types are dolmens and menhirs.**
- **menhir (from Breton *men*, "stone," and *hir*, "long"): prehistoric monument consisting of a single block of vertically standing stone.**
- **ritual: all the religious practices and ceremonies carried out within the framework of a belief or religion.**

The name "prehistory" is given to the period before people knew how to read or write. History as such begins around 3000 B.C., with the invention of writing. From paintings and bones discovered in caves, we know something of the **ritual** and religious practices of prehistoric people living long before that time.

The first graves
The simple burying of the dead is a religious act, since it implies that the human body has needs beyond those of everyday life. The

two skeletons of children buried in the Grimaldi cave, France, around 30,000 B.C.

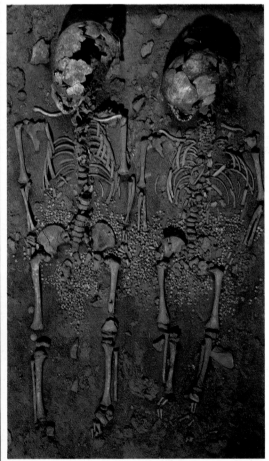

most ancient traces of religious beliefs are human remains, surrounded or covered in objects and buried in pits. These pits, which can be regarded as the first graves, date from the time of the Neanderthals, who lived 80,000 years ago, and have been discovered in Europe and the Middle East. Later, between 40,000 and 10,000 B.C., in the time of our own species, *Homo sapiens sapiens*, graves became more numerous. The dead were buried in pits, the walls of which were covered by a red clay called red ocher. The bodies were decked out with jewels, pearls, and shell and ivory pendants and were surrounded with all sorts of objects, including weapons and tools of stone or bone. Although the exact meaning of these funeral practices remains unknown, the special treatment given to the dead shows a preoccupation with what would happen after death.

Sculptures and cave paintings
The appearance of the first art forms occurs in the same period, beginning 30,000 years ago, and they seem to have religious significance. They are sculptures carved in bone and stone, statuettes of women with breasts, buttocks, and sexual organs greatly exaggerated in size. They may represent **fertility** goddesses. Also, in western Europe, around 150 caves have been discovered that are decorated with paintings or engravings from this period representing geometrical forms, hands, and, in particular, animals. Cave artists painted horses, bison, deer, mammoths, and rhinoceroses. The meaning of these paintings is a mystery. We can only surmise that in a period when hunting played a central role in human life, animals were both feared and sought after and so were an important part in human beliefs. Moreover,

cave at Perito Moreno, Argentina, decorated with hand paintings

A painted bison in the Altamira cave, Spain

of rubble, called **cairns**, or earthen mounds, known as **barrows**. **Menhirs** are standing stones. They can be single, aligned, or arranged in a circle as in the case of Stonehenge in England or Carnac in France.
☐

the fact that access to these caves is often very difficult may suggest that they were not dwellings but had a religious function.

Dolmens and menhirs

From 8000 B.C., living patterns began to change. People settled in villages and no longer lived solely from hunting and gathering but began to farm and to domesticate animals. This is known as the neolithic period. The transformation in the way of life brought about important changes in religious beliefs and practices. Many female statuettes from this period have been found—seemingly dedicated to the **cult** of the Earth, the Sun, and the cycle of the seasons, with the intention of bringing about plentiful harvests. In this period in many regions, and in particular in western Europe, monuments called **megaliths** were constructed from enormous blocks of stone. Megaliths built in the form of a giant table are known as **dolmens**. They were collective **graves** protected either by mounds

fertility goddess found at Çatal Huyük, Turkey, 6th–5th century B.C.

The site of Stonehenge in Britain

This monument was built between 2000 and 1500 B.C., which places it at the end of the neolithic period. The standing stones form two concentric circles, the larger of which is 32 m (105 ft.) in diameter. Within these circles, two horseshoe-shaped ovals surround a large stone that was undoubtedly also a standing stone. This stone shows the point on the horizon where the sun rises at the summer solstice. Two smaller stones, at the southeast and northeast, indicate the sunrise at the winter solstice. Historians conjecture that Stonehenge was built for the cult of a sun god. Stonehenge was in use as a ceremonial center until 800 B.C. Most of the menhirs collapsed over the centuries, but in modern times, some have been rebuilt and their tops surmounted by transverse slabs.

11

Mesopotamia

The religion of Mesopotamia is the oldest known. Archaeologists have discovered clay tablets on which the Mesopotamians engraved the stories of their gods.

- **astrology:** studying how the position of heavenly bodies is believed to influence events and the behavior and destiny of humans.
- **city-state:** a small independent state made up of a city and its surrounding countryside. Each city-state had its own laws.
- **cult:** worship rendered to a god or a deity: ceremony in which the worship is rendered.
- **deity:** divine being, a god or goddess.
- **divination:** the practice of foretelling the future by interpreting specific phenomena as signs sent by the gods.
- **offering:** gift made to a deity, such as food, incense, goods, jewels.
- **scribe (from Latin *scribere*, "to write"):** a person responsible for writing out texts, who played an important role in the city-states.
- **symbolize:** to represent an idea using an object or a person.
- **temple:** religious building consecrated to the cult of a deity.

Between 3000 and 300 B.C. in Mesopotamia (a region that roughly corresponds to modern Iraq), large cities such as Sumer, Ur, Akkad, and Babylon emerged and prospered. It was there that writing was invented around 3000 B.C. A great number of texts have survived, telling us of these peoples' religious beliefs and practices. Initially, each Mesopotamian city-state had its own patron gods. Over time, the gods of the more powerful cities were imposed on the whole region.

Gods and goddesses

The Mesopotamian gods are numerous, each playing a role in the organization of the universe. The god An (or Anu) is the creator of the sky and the universe, but he assigns power to his son, Enlil, who is lord of the wind and sovereign god of the universe. The god of water, Enki (or Ea), is endowed with great wisdom. For this reason, both gods and humans appeal to him in situations of great difficulty. These three principal gods are surrounded by many other deities, such as Adad, the god of storms, or Shamash, the sun god. In Babylon around 2000 B.C., Enlil was supplanted by his son, Marduk, a younger but all-powerful god. Goddesses are almost as numerous as the gods. The most powerful was Inanna-Ishtar, goddess of love and fertility and

also of war. People believed that the gods resembled them: gods are imagined with human faces, and they eat, drink, fall in love, and marry. They quarrel, lie, and sometimes fight. However, they are immortal and all-powerful, and their intelligence is far superior to that of the humans they have created to serve them.

The creation of man

A Mesopotamian poem engraved on clay tablets tells how the gods decided to create humankind. A very long time ago, heavenly society was made up of the Annunaku and the Igugu. The Annunaku did nothing, while the Igugu worked to feed them. One day, the Igugu rebelled and refused to continue with their work. The gods then held a meeting and decided to create human beings, who were destined to serve them and to procure for them everything necessary and agreeable. This myth shows that, for the Mesopotamians, the gods are masters of human destiny. Evils such as war, famine, or disease are manifestations of their anger. For this reason, human beings try to win their favor by building **temples** and creating a **cult** for them.

a man in an attitude of prayer, 3rd century B.C.

bulls guarding a gate in Iraq dedicated to the goddess Ishtar

Divination and astrology

The Mesopotamian priests studied and practiced **divination**, the art of determining the will of the gods. This they did by interpreting exceptional events, such as an outbreak of disease or the birth of a malformed child. **Astrology**, which originated in Mesopotamia, was also a way of finding out about divine decisions. Any change in the movement or the usual appearance of the heavenly bodies (sun, moon, stars, or planets) was considered to be a message sent from the gods. □

The Ancient Middle East

The different religions of Mesopotamia, "the land between the rivers" (the Tigris and the Euphrates); Egypt; and Persia (present-day Iran) all influenced each other.

The religion of the Hittites

The kingdom of the Hittites flourished between 1650 and 1200 B.C., in Anatolia, a region of Asia corresponding to modern Turkey. The Hittites worshiped several gods, including this warrior god. The most important divinity was Arinna, goddess of the sun, who reigned over the other gods. More than 30 temples have been found in the capital, Hattusas. The cult was organized around the royal court, for the kings were also priests.

The god Adad and the goddess Ishtar (9th century B.C.)

The ziggurat and the priests

To honor the gods, the Mesopotamians built numerous temples known as ziggurats. These are towerlike buildings in several tiers. They have a monumental stairway that **symbolizes** their role, the creation of a link between the sky and earth. At the top is the shrine that shelters the statue of the god. The oldest ziggurats date from the beginning of the second millennium B.C. Usually built of brick, most are now in a poor state of preservation. The priests were learned men—and usually **scribes**—responsible for seeing that ritual was properly observed. Each day, at the foot of the statue, they left **offerings** that the local people brought such as food, incense, precious clothing, and jewels.

the moon-god Sin, shown on an Assyrian bas-relief of the 8th century B.C.

The temples built by the ancient Egyptians to honor their gods still stand today along the banks of the Nile. The Egyptians also raised pyramids to house the mummies of their pharaohs.

Egyptian religion

embalm: to treat a corpse with substances (aromatics, salts, resins) that prevent it from decomposing.

mastaba: bench-shaped tomb of the first pharaohs, and later of high dignitaries, of Egypt.

mummy: corpse preserved after being embalmed and wrapped in bandages.

naos: the room inside a temple where the statue of the god stood.

pharaoh: a king of ancient Egypt, considered a god by the Egyptians.

pyramid: large monument that served as a tomb for the pharaohs. The first Egyptian pyramid was built around 2600 B.C. at Saqqara.

reincarnation: coming back to life after death in a different body.

sacrifice: offering made to a deity, usually by killing animals.

sarcophagus: a coffin in which the Egyptians placed a mummy.

sphinx: a monster with a lion's body and a human head.

For more than 3,000 years (from 3200 B.C. to 30 B.C.), Egyptian civilization flourished in a sun-baked desert landscape. In the narrow valley made fertile by the floods of the Nile, powerful cities were united under the authority of one king, the **pharaoh**. Among their many gods the Egyptians included the pharaoh, who was regarded as a living god. Priests at his command were responsible to the gods in each temple. They also directed the ceremonies for the dead, which were of primary importance in their religion.

from left to right, the gods Horus and Osiris and the goddess Isis (8th century B.C.)

The Egyptian gods

Each region and city worshiped distinct gods. However, the principal gods were recognized by all. Amun-Re, the sun god, is one of the most important gods. Wearing the solar disc on his head, he is born each morning and disappears each evening. All day, he sails in his golden boat across the ocean of the sky. According to legend, Osiris was the first king of Egypt. His brother Seth murders him and cuts his body into fourteen pieces, which Seth scatters all over Egypt. Isis, Osiris' wife, finds the pieces one by one, puts the body together, wraps it in bandages, and revives her husband. Osiris is thus the first **mummy** and becomes the god of the dead. Besides a sorceress, Isis is the goddess of life, the Divine Mother. Horus is the son of Osiris and Isis. He avenges his father by regaining the throne of Egypt from Seth. Horus is the hawk-god, the protector of the pharaoh. Around 1360 B.C., the pharaoh Amenophis IV tried to impose one god, Aton, a god of the sun. He himself took the name of Akhenaton (adorer of the sun). After his death, the old religion was restored, for the Egyptians were strongly attached to their traditional gods.

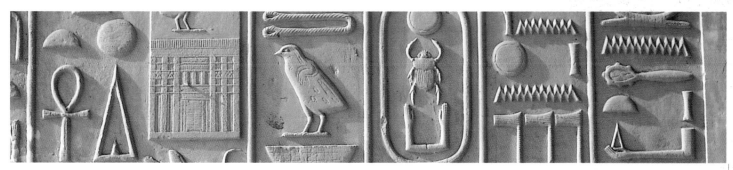

The sun god Re (or Ra) sends down his rays in the form of lotus flowers.

The pharaoh

King of Egypt, the pharaoh was considered at one and the same time the supreme priest and a living god among men. For this reason, it was not permitted to look at his face. The Egyptians thought that he was a descendant of the first legendary king of Egypt, Osiris, and the **reincarnation** of Horus on earth, and that after his death, he would return to the kingdom of the gods. The pharaoh guaranteed the order of the world. Thanks to him, the cycle of the Nile floods and harvests was repeated each year. The pharaoh was the religious leader, and in principle, he alone was empowered to appeal to the gods in the temples. However, he delegated his powers to priests, for he could not be present each day in every temple.

The temples

The temples were the homes of the gods, built on the banks of the Nile with their facades always parallel to the river. A long avenue lined with **sphinxes** led to the monumental entrance. Within was a courtyard where people were allowed to assemble only during major festivals. At the back of the courtyard was the entrance to a columned hall where **sacrifices** were offered during ceremonies. Deep within the temple, in a small but magnificently adorned room, was the god's dwelling place, the **naos**, containing his statue. Only the pharaoh and the priests were permitted to enter this sanctuary.

The priests

Each temple had several priests under the direction of a chief priest. The priests had to be able to read and write. Their duties were passed down from father to son. They formed a rich and powerful social group, for they collected the taxes owed to the gods. Priests shaved their heads and wore long robes. They took care of the god to whom their temple was consecrated. Since the god was supposed to live in the statue that represented him, each morning the priests would awake the statue. They would wash, perfume, dress, and feed it, and then leave offerings at its feet.□

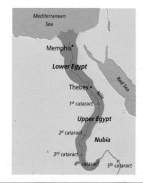

Anubis, the jackal-headed god

The god Bes

Bes is an ugly misshapen dwarf, but his ugliness made him useful to humans. His

grimacing face put evil to flight. The Egyptians placed great value on this god and affixed a statue of Bes to the doors of their houses.

Ancient Egypt

As the pharaohs became more powerful, they extended their empire farther south toward Nubia.

a funeral procession

The afterlife

painted wooden model of a boat found in the tomb
of Tutankhamun, about 1350 B.C.

Mummification

First the entrails were taken out of the corpse, which was then saturated for forty days in a salt, natron, to dry it. The embalming priest then stuffed the corpse with resins and aromatic herbs. Then the corpse was rubbed down with oils and ointments, wrapped in a shroud, and bound with thin linen bandages, while a priest read out prayers. Several shrouds were often placed over each other. Inside the shroud, objects were placed in specific places to provide magical protection. The face was made up and sometimes fitted with enamel eyes, which gave it a lifelike appearance.

The Egyptians believed people lived on after death. The journey from the kingdom of the living to the kingdom of the dead was dangerous, so the dead were protected by rituals and prayers. Tombs were designed as living quarters, with all the furniture and objects the deceased would need in the next life. However, the dead person first had to pass the dreaded test of the judgment of Osiris.

The funeral rites

The dead person could only experience a new life in the beyond if the body was preserved. To this end, it was necessary to embalm the body, to transform it into a mummy. A mask painted in the likeness of the dead person covered the face. The mummy was then placed in three **sarcophaguses**, which fitted one into the other. They were shaped like the body of the deceased, and the outer one was painted in his or her likeness. Items needed for everyday life, including food, toiletries, jewels, and weapons were placed near the sarcophagus. Statuettes or "shawabtis" represented servants, who would work for the dead person in the afterlife. Rich persons took up to 365 shawabtis with them, so that they would have a servant for every day of the year.

The tombs

To protect their bodies and the riches that they took to the afterlife, the pharaohs had giant tombs built on the west bank of the Nile. This was regarded as the bank of the dead because the sun sets on that side of the river. The tombs of the first pharaohs were low, rectangular buildings called **mastabas**. A mastaba encloses a deep well that leads to the chamber where the deceased lay. Above this is the chamber of offerings. When the pharaohs decided to build **pyramids**, mastabas became the tombs of the kingdom's high dignitaries. The first pyramids were stepped, such as that of Joser at Saqqara, symbolizing a gigantic staircase leading to the home of the gods. Later the

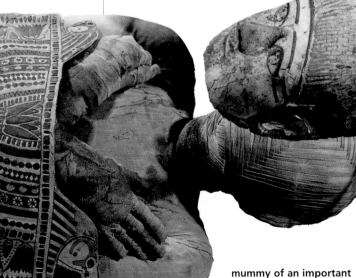

mummy of an important
Egyptian of the 3rd–2nd
century B.C.

a priest presenting offerings to a dead person

four sides were made smooth to symbolize a sun ray, like the sides of the pyramid of Cheops. Inside, a long sloping gallery leads to what amounts to complete living quarters made up of several rooms separated by sealed doors that surround the chamber holding the sarcophagus and contain the riches of the dead king. A system of galleries and empty rooms was meant to mislead thieves, but almost all the tombs have been plundered since the time of the pharaohs.

Around 1500 B.C. (known as hypogeas) the pharaohs chose to have tombs hollowed out from the steep walls of the mountains facing the city of Thebes, in the Valley of the Kings. Like the mastabas, the tombs contain a **cult** chamber that comprises several huge rooms decorated with bas-reliefs and paintings. A secret well leads to the sarcophagus chamber. The more modest tombs are wells 5 m (16 ft.) deep, at the bottom of which is a chamber just big enough to accommodate the coffin, inside which the corpse was not mummified. As for the poor, they were simply rolled up in a mat and buried in the sand with a few personal objects.

The judgment of Osiris

The Egyptians believed that after death the dead set out on a long journey to the kingdom of Osiris (or the kingdom of the dead), where they had to appear before a court. The Book of the Dead, a collection of spells, was left in the sarcophagus to help the dead person reply to Osiris' interrogation concerning the person's deeds while alive. Then the soul of the deceased was weighed: the heart was put on one side of a pair of scales and a feather on the other. If the scales balanced, the dead person gained entry to the kingdom of Osiris. If not, the dead person was devoured by a monster and disappeared forever. ☐

A Canopic vase

The entrails and brain, considered necessary for the next life, were extracted from the corpse. They were kept in Canopic vases that were put with the dead in the tomb. The lid of the vase usually represents one of the four sons of Horus, here the hawk Kebehsenuf.

The pyramids of Giza

These pyramids near Cairo are those of the pharaohs Cheops, Khephren, and Mykerinus. They are the largest ever built. In front of them are three pyramids of queens.

The weighing of the soul

In Egyptian belief, the deceased (on the right, dressed in white) went after death to the kingdom of the dead to be judged before a court for both the good and bad actions committed during life. His soul was weighed on the scales of a balance: if too heavy, he would be devoured by the monster of the underworld. If it was light, he would remain eternally in the kingdom of the dead. Here, the court is made up of the gods Horus (seated on the left), Anubis the jackal god, and Thoth, the ibis god, who is keeping count. Usually, the god Osiris, easily recognized by his greenish color, presides over the court.

The ancient Greeks wrote many stories that tell of their gods. To worship them, the Greeks would assemble at vast sanctuaries where they organized major festivals.

The religion of the Gre

- **acropolis:** the highest part of the cities of ancient Greece. The most famous is the Acropolis of Athens, on which magnificent temples were built in the 5th century B.C.
- **altar:** table or surface on which offerings to deities are placed or sacrifices are made.
- **city-state:** small independent state made up of a city and its surrounding countryside. Each city-state had its own laws.
- **hero:** a mythological character to whom extraordinary deeds were attributed.
- **libation:** offering to a deity of a liquid poured over the ground or over an altar.
- **pentathlon:** contest of five sporting events.
- **shrine:** building consecrated to religious ceremonies; a holy place.

From 600 B.C., rival independent city-states such as Athens and Sparta emerged in Greece. In spite of their political differences, these states shared the same beliefs. These beliefs consist of a body of marvellous tales, or myths, which explain the origins of the world and of humans and recount the adventures of the gods and goddesses.

The myths and the texts

At first, myths were not written down. The storytellers, or bards, learned them by heart and sang them in public to the accompaniment of a lyre. The poet Homer, in the 9th or 8th century B.C., may have been the first to put down in writing the ancient legends. Two very famous texts are attributed to him, the *Iliad* and the *Odyssey*, both major sources of information on the beliefs of the Greeks. The *Iliad* tells the story of the war between the Greeks and the city of Troy (thought to be in modern Turkey). During this war,

some gods sided with the Greeks and others supported the Trojans. Thus they quarrel through the intermediary of humans, and the humans' fate depends on their will. The *Odyssey* recounts the return of the **hero** Odysseus to his homeland when the war with Troy is over. Hounded by certain gods but protected by Athena, he takes ten years to return home, after many adventures during which he encounters the cyclops Polyphemus, the sorceress Circe, the Sirens, the nymph Calypso, and the beautiful Nausicaa.

The creation of the world

The Greeks explained the creation of the world as the action of the gods. In the beginning Chaos gives birth to Gaia, the earth, who brings to life the mountains and the sky, Uranus. Then Gaia unites with Uranus and gives birth to the Titans, giants who are the first masters of the universe. The

The Greek temple of Segesta in Italy dates from the 5th century B.C.

Dionysus holding a cup and Hephaestos riding a mule

The twelve gods of Olympus

Hera · Zeus · Poseidon · Demeter

Athena · Aphrodite · Artemis · Dionysus · Hephaestos · Ares · Hermes · Apollo

Heracles and the centaur Nessus

The centaur Nessus, a monster half-horse and half-man, offended Deianira, the wife of Heracles, who decided to kill him. As he dies, Nessus gives his blood-soaked tunic to Deianira and tells her that if Heracles wears it he will always be a faithful husband. But when Heracles puts it on, he dies in agony.

Ancient Greece

The Greek world was more extensive than Greece itself: it included the cities of Asia Minor and numerous colonies founded from the 8th century B.C. throughout the Mediterranean.

Titan Cronos devours all his children, except Zeus, the last, who is saved by his mother. When he grows up, Zeus revolts against his father and forces him to spit out his brothers and sisters, and together they fight the Titans. They are victorious, and Zeus becomes the king of the gods. According to another myth, a Titan named Prometheus creates man from clay and water.

The gods of Olympus

The twelve principal gods dwell on Olympus, the highest mountain in Greece. They form a family under the authority of Zeus, the lord of the sky. With him live his wife Hera, the goddess of marriage, and numerous offspring: Athena, goddess of wisdom, arts, and sciences, born fully armed from the head of Zeus; Apollo, god of the sun; Aphrodite, goddess of love; Ares, god of war; Artemis, goddess of hunting; and Hermes, messenger of the gods. Other gods of Olympus are brothers and sisters of Zeus, such as Hephaestos, god of fire and smiths; Poseidon, god of the sea, who lives at the bottom of the oceans; and Hades, the god of the underworld and of the dead, who lives under the earth. The Greeks believed that the gods had a human appearance, and they venerated their statues. The Greeks attributed the passions, qualities, and faults of mere mortals to them. The gods often quarrel, but they also have large banquets at which they feed on ambrosia and nectar, substances that make them immortal. Unlike humans, the gods are immortal and all-powerful. At any opportunity, they may intervene in the lives of men.

The heroes

The heroes, usually the son of a god and a mortal, accomplish extraordinary deeds with the help of the gods. The most famous of all is Heracles (Hercules), son of Zeus and a mortal. He has superhuman strength and carries out twelve incredible exploits (the twelve labors). These included strangling the lion that ravaged the region of Nemea in Peloponnesus, cleaning out the immense stables of Augeas, and chaining up Cerberus, the monstrous three-headed dog and guardian of the underworld. □

the sanctuary of Delphi in Greece, 6th century B.C.

The major sanctuaries and festivals

The Pythia of Delphi

The Greeks went to Delphi to honor the god Apollo and to ask for his advice. His reply, or oracle, was given by a woman called the Pythia. Seated on a three-legged stool, she would answer the questions of advice-seekers by crying out and uttering meaningless words. The priests interpreted the Pythia's reply.

Greek religion was based on practices and rituals that accompanied all the important acts of public and private life. Prayers, offerings, **libations**, animal sacrifices, processions, sporting and artistic competitions were, for the Greeks, the many ways of obtaining aid from the gods and of thanking them for their protection.

Public and private worship

Each city honored its patron god, to whom a temple was consecrated: this was the public cult. Citizens elected or chosen by lot fulfilled the duties of priests. Any citizen could be a priest, as no special training was necessary. The priest responsible for the public cult organized the festivals and ceremonies. Ceremonies always took place outside, near the temple. There, the priest would sacrifice oxen, pigs, or goats adorned with garlands and burn a part of the animal's flesh on an **altar**. The private cult was practiced in each house, on a small altar on which the sacred flame was always kept burning. Each morning the father of the family offered libations: as he recited prayers, he would pour over the ground some drops of wine, milk, or honey. At the beginning of each meal, he offered bread, fruit, vegetables, or cakes to Hestia, goddess of the hearth. It was to Hestia that a husband would present the wife he had just married, a newborn baby, or a new slave.

The great sanctuaries

Originally, the Greeks built small temples in places that they held to be sacred. This might be a spring where a goddess had bathed or a wood where a god had rested. As time passed, thanks to the offerings of the faithful, the building would expand and other temples would be built nearby. In some cases, as at Epidaurus, a theater would be built for performances to honor the gods. In fact, it was the Greeks who began dramatic performances of tragedies and comedies, which were financed by rich citizens. On set dates, festivals took place at the sanctuaries, where Greeks from different cities would assemble. They came from all over the country: to Olympia to honor Zeus, to Delphi to celebrate Apollo,

race between quadrigas, chariots drawn by four horses

The Greek theater at Epidaurus (4th century B.C.).

and to Epidaurus to pray to the healer god Asclepius, son of Apollo. Festivals included singing and poetry contests, as at Delphi, and sporting events.

boxers training

The Olympic games

From 776 B.C., a sporting festival known as the games, which also included musical and literary competitions, took place over seven days in the summer every four years at Olympia in honor of Zeus and his consort Hera. Women were not allowed to participate or to attend. A month before the start of the games, an Olympic truce was proclaimed, during which peace reigned over the cities. The competitors could then go to Olympia without risk. The stadium accommodated a large crowd, estimated at about 20,000 spectators. There were ten sports for adults (including running, wrestling, boxing, **pentathlon,** and chariot racing) and three for youths: running, wrestling, and boxing. The winners were awarded a crown of olive branches and welcomed with great honors on their return to their city.

The Panathenaea

The patron goddess of Athens was Athena, after whom the city was named. Her statue stood in the city's largest temple, the Parthenon, situated on the **Acropolis**. Each year in July, and more solemnly every four years, the whole population honored Athena during the Panathenaea festival. For this occasion, a tunic (the peplos) was woven for nine months by young girls aged from 7 to 12 to clothe the statue of Athena. Then the peplos was carried in procession from the city to the top of the Acropolis, to Athena's temple. At the head of the procession walked the magistrates and priests, then the elderly bearing olive branches. Women came next, carrying baskets of offerings. Horsemen brought up the rear of the procession. The festival ended with a great sacrifice of animals. ☐

Sacrifice of a pig

Sacrifice was the act that linked humans to gods. The offering consisted of meat, which was a luxury in Greece. Part of the roast flesh was burned entirely as food for the gods, and the rest was eaten by the worshipers.

Athletes racing

In the palaestra, a public place found in all Greek cities, citizens trained for the sports practiced in honor of the gods. They wore very little: the word *gymnastics* comes from the Greek *gymnos*, which means "naked."

The religion of the Ror

- **augur:** priest who interpreted omens, such as the flight of birds or the appetite of sacred chickens, to divine the will of the gods.
- **cult:** worship rendered to a god or a deity: ceremony in which that worship is rendered.
- **deify:** to regard as a god.
- **genius:** a divinity who protected a particular person or place.
- **haruspex (plural haruspices):** priest who examined animal entrails, especially livers, to discover the will of the gods.
- **lar (plural lares):** patron god of the hearth. Lares also protected crossroads.
- **lararium:** altar located within the house, intended for the cult of the lares.
- **manes:** souls of the dead, considered to be divinities.
- **omen:** a sign thought to reveal the will of the gods or the future.
- **penates:** deities protecting the home, specifically the storerooms and furniture.
- **ritual:** the religious practices and ceremonies carried out within the framework of a belief or religion.
- **soothsayer:** person who claims to be able to read the future and to carry out divination.

At its founding in the 8th century B.C., Rome was no more than a village. Later, it became a powerful city that, during the 2nd and 1st centuries B.C., conquered Greece, Asia Minor, Judaea, Spain, and Gaul. Rome then became an immense empire that endured until the barbarian invasions of the 5th century A.D. The Roman religion spread throughout the conquered peoples but also borrowed a great deal from them.

The domestic cult

The first gods venerated by the Romans were those that protected the family. Accordingly, each family honored the deities of the house, and in the presence of the father, who was considered a priest, carried out numerous rites in

front of the domestic altar known as the **lararium**. Each day offerings to the god protecting the hearth, the **lar**, were placed on the altar: a little wine, bread, fruit. On the eve of their marriage, young girls offered it their dolls to show that their childhood had ended. The **penates** watched over the furniture and storerooms, while a **genius** protected the father of the family, whose prayers and offerings were intended to ward off thieves and bad luck. Lastly, the **manes**, representing the spirits of the ancestors, were also worshiped.

A domestic altar, or lararium, from Pompeii in Italy; the genius protecting the father of the family is depicted between two lares.

an altar of the lares in a house in Pompeii, Italy

ans

Roman gods and Greek gods

When they became masters of Greece, the Romans established links between their gods and those of the Greeks by changing their names and sometimes changing their roles. The principal Roman gods are Jupiter (Greek Zeus), Juno (Hera), Neptune (Poseidon), Venus (Aphrodite), Minerva (Athena), Mercury (Hermes), Vulcan (Hephaestos), Ceres (Demeter), Bacchus (Dionysus), Apollo (Apollo), Mars (Ares), and Diana (Artemis).

The imperial cult

In the 1st century B.C., after Augustus attained power, the person of the emperor became sacred, and a cult was devoted to him throughout the whole Roman empire. The month of August (*Augustus* in Latin) was dedicated to him, and on the first day of the month, major festivals took place. The emperor was honored by the building of temples and carving of statues in his image. On his death, the senate or law-making assembly **deified** him. From then on, his name would be associated with that of Jupiter. From the second half of the 1st century A.D., emperors sought to be acknowledged as gods during their lifetime: Nero identified himself with Apollo and Commodus with Hercules. Across the Roman empire, statues "of Rome and of Augustus" were raised. All citizens were obliged to practice the imperial cult.

The priests

All the priests were under the orders of the *pontifex maximus* or high priest (a title reserved for the emperor from the time of

An augur, recognizable by his staff and a sacred chicken.

Augustus in the 1st century B.C.). Appointed for life, the high priest set the calendar for the festivals during which chariot races and combats between gladiators took place. He also decided the favorable days on which work was permitted and the inauspicious days when the gods forbade all activity. Women also played an important role as vestal virgins. In a temple at Rome consecrated to the goddess Vesta, guardian of the sacred flame, the vestal virgins were responsible for maintaining the fire. Recruited at the age of ten, they had to fulfill their duties for thirty years and were not allowed to marry. Before undertaking any important action, the Romans sought to know the will of the gods. For this purpose, **soothsayers** known as **haruspices** examined the entrails of sacrificed animals. Other priests or **augurs** observed the flights of birds across the sky, the shape of the clouds, or the appetite of sacred chickens: all these were **omens** that the augurs were responsible for interpreting. □

The Roman empire

By the 3rd century A.D. the Roman empire extended all around the Mediterranean.

The Etruscans

The Etruscans dominated central Italy before the Romans. They passed on to their successors, the Romans, the art of divining the will of the gods. The Etruscans believed that the dead went on living a calm, peaceful life. Spouses, as shown in this sarcophagus of about 520 B.C., were sometimes buried together.

Many warrior peoples lived beyond the Greek and Roman world. These included the Scythians, the Celts, the Germans, and the Slavs, who roamed across the great plains of northern and central Europe.

Nomadic peoples

- **altar:** table or surface on which offerings to deities are placed or sacrifices are made.
- **druid:** among the Celts, priests who also fulfilled the role of teacher, judge, and arbiter between peoples and, sometimes, of soothsayer. Each year, they gathered sacred mistletoe from oak trees. Druids were few in number and enjoyed immense prestige.
- **fertility:** quality of being able to reproduce, of being able to have children. In ancient religious beliefs the earth's fertility was compared to a woman's fertility.
- **funeral:** solemn ceremony of burial.
- **funeral rite:** religious practices and ceremonies carried out in honor of the dead.
- **nomadic:** describes a person with no fixed home who moves from one place to another.
- **offering:** gift made to a deity. This may be food, perfumes, goods, jewels, and so on.
- **soothsayer:** person who claims to be able to read the future and to carry out divination.

The peoples of northern and central Europe left no written records, for their culture was passed on by word of mouth. What we know about them mostly comes from accounts by Greeks and Romans and from later Christian writers of the Middle Ages. We also have some information about the religions they practiced from objects found in archaeological digs; these tell us in particular about their **funeral rites**.

The Scythians

It is thought that around the 12th century B.C., the people called the Scythians lived between the rivers Danube and Don, in the south of what is today Russia. During the 3rd century B.C., the Scythians were driven out by other **nomadic** tribes and settled on the shores of the Black Sea. Feared warriors, the Scythians roamed across the steppes on their small horses. They were nomads, moving with their flocks in search of rich pastures. They had no altars, temples, or statues to honor their gods, chief of whom was the sky-father Papa, consort of the earth-mother Api. They also venerated the goddess of fire, Tabiti, and the god of war, represented by a sword planted in a pile of brushwood. Animals, mainly horses, were offered to the gods as sacrifices. The Scythians believed that people had souls that lived on after death. For the **funerals** of their warrior chiefs, they held elaborate

ceremonies. The tribal leader was buried with his horses in a wooden chamber. Weapons, golden jewels, meat, and wine for the last journey were placed around the corpse. The tomb was then covered with an enormous earthen mound, known as a tumulus or barrow.

The Celts

The Celts originated mainly in southern Germany, spreading during the first millennium B.C. over the whole of western Europe and into the Balkans and Asia Minor. However, between the 3rd and 1st centuries B.C., first the Germans and then the Romans overcame them. Of the ancient Celtic kingdoms, only those in Ireland, where the Celts settled in the 5th century B.C., remained untouched. The Celts believed in numerous gods, often grouped in families. The gods of the Celts of Gaul (France) and those of the Irish Celts resemble each other, although they often bear different names. Thus the god representing light, air, life, and death is called Taranis in Gaul and Dagda in Ireland. Brigit, "the shining one," a goddess of the Irish Celts and daughter of Dagda, is the equivalent of Epona, mounted goddess of war and wisdom, venerated in Gaul. A special place was accorded for Lugh, the supreme god, and for Cernunnos, the stag-horned god, symbol of **fertility**. Religious rites were carried

a god with a wild boar from Celtic Gaul

Celtic god with a wheel and mythical animals

Europe

out by the druids, who were priests, wise men, healers, teachers, and **soothsayers**. Their knowledge was passed on in long poems, which they learned by heart.

the god Thor

The Germans

The ancient Germans migrated from southern Scandinavia in the 1st and 2nd centuries A.D. to the center and north of Europe. What is known of their beliefs comes from the Roman historian Tacitus (writing in the 1st century) and from legends of the Middle Ages. The Scandinavians, or Vikings, were descendants of the Germanic peoples of northern Europe and believed in the same gods. These Nordic gods have points in common with the Celtic gods. The Germanic peoples distinguished two groups of deities: the Aesir, sovereign and warrior gods, and the Vanir, gods of fertility and crafts. The most powerful god is Odin (or Wotan, which means "fury"), the god of war and poetry, who belongs to the Aesir family. Thor, or Donar ("thunder"), armed with a hammer, is the god of lightning. The god Tyr represents justice. Odin's wife, Frigg, is one of the Vanir and is the goddess of marriage and childbirth. All the gods dwell in Asgard, a mountain at the center of the world. They are usually represented gathered in a court at the foot of the great ash tree, Yggdrasil, which supports the world. During festivals, the Germans honored their gods by banquets and animal

sacrifices. There were no priests; usually it was the tribal chief who organized and directed the sacrifices.

The Slavs

The Slavs divide up into different groups. Originally from Poland and Russia, they spread across eastern Europe in the 1st century A.D. The cult of nature and of the dead seems to have been the basis of their religion, which was centered on specific gods. Perun, who among the Russians was the god of thunder and lightning, was known as Stantevit by the western Slavs. The Slavs believed that nature was full of numerous spirits that intervened in everyday life. □

The nomadic peoples of Europe

Warrior peoples living in western and northern Europe migrated at various times during the past.

The Trundholm chariot

Made around 1650 B.C., this miniature chariot made of gold-plated bronze was found in Denmark, well preserved by the peat in which it was buried. A horse pulls the disc of the sun. This proves that the Germanic people practiced some form of sun worship.

The Mayas, Aztecs, and Incas of Central and South America left an impressive legacy of religious monuments that indicate the great importance of religion among these peoples.

Mayas, Aztecs, and

astrology: a practice that consists in studying the influence of the position of heavenly bodies on terrestrial events and on the behavior and destiny of men.

astronomy: study of the universe and its constitution, and of the position, movement, and nature of the stars.

city-state: a small independent state made up of a city and its surrounding countryside. Each city-state had its own laws.

cult: worship rendered to a god or deity; ceremony in which that worship is rendered.

libation: offering to a deity of a liquid poured over the ground or over an altar.

offering: gift made to a deity. This may be food, scents, goods, jewels, etc.

pre-Columbian: existing in America before the arrival of Christopher Columbus in 1492.

sacrifice: offering made to a deity, often by killing animals.

The civilizations that existed in America before the arrival of Christopher Columbus in 1492 are referred to as **pre-Columbian**. Of these civilizations, the most advanced and wealthy flourished in Central America and in the Andes mountains. The principal empires were those of the Mayas, the Aztecs, and the Incas. With the Spanish conquest of the 16th century, these civilizations disappeared. The customs and beliefs of the three peoples, who lived by farming, had points in common. They worshiped the elemental forces of

Mayan funeral mask dating from the 7th century A.D.

nature, such as the sun, the moon, rain, and thunder. Priests were very powerful and played an important role, since they possessed knowledge of mathematics, **astronomy, astrology,** and medicine. They drew up precise calendars and directed ceremonies in the temples that dominated the city-states. The survival of the soul after death is another belief shared by these peoples, who feared and respected the dead.

The Mayas

The oldest advanced pre-Columbian civilization is that of the Mayas, which lasted from the 3rd to the 10th century A.D. Their territory originally extended over a large part of Central America: from the Yucatán peninsula to modern Guatemala and Honduras. The Mayas were organized in independent city-states and did not create a large empire like those of the Aztecs or the Incas. Little is known about their religion. However, the Mayan gods were numerous and related to natural phenomena. Represented in half-human, half-animal forms, they are either beneficent or malevolent. The principal deities are Hunabku, the father of the gods; Itzamna, the king of the sky and chief god of the priests, who taught humans about writing and the calendar; and his companion Ixchel, the mother goddess.

The Aztecs

The Aztecs were formerly nomads from the northwest of Mexico. In the 12th century, they settled in the valley of Mexico, where in the 14th century they founded their capital of Tenochtitlán (today Mexico City). They conquered the neighboring peoples and established a vast empire. The principal Aztec gods were

detail from an Aztec calendar

ncas

Quetzalcoatl, god of light, who brought civilization to humans; Tezcatlipoca, god of night, winter and death; Huitzilopochtli, the sun-god and god of war; Tlaloc, god of rain and thunder; Chicomecoatl, goddess of corn (maize); and Tlazolteotl, goddess of love. The Aztecs believed that the universe created by the gods was being destroyed gradually over time. To prevent the world from disappearing again and to make the sun reappear each day, they thought it necessary to offer the gods human blood. Thus, human **sacrifice** was the basis of the Aztec religion. They fought ceaselessly, making war on their neighbors to supply the captives whose still-beating hearts were torn out as sacrifices to the gods.

The Incas

In the 13th century, the Incas of the high plateaus of Peru in South America conquered their neighbors and began to rule an immense territory. By the beginning of the 16th century, the Inca empire was a highly organized state, with an all-powerful emperor, known as the Inca. The emperor was believed to be the son of the sun-god, Inti, and a god in his own right. The Incas placed Inti at the center of their religion and imposed his cult on conquered peoples. Both the coronation and death of the emperor were the occasion for major ceremonies involving **libations** of beer, sacrifices of llamas and sometimes even of children. The Incas also placed special emphasis on the cult of their ancestors. ☐

overview of the ancient Inca city of
Machu Picchu in Peru

The god Quetzalcoatl

This Aztec god was man, snake, and bird in one body. When the Spanish conquistadors arrived wearing feathered helmets, the Aztecs believed that they were reincarnations of Quetzalcoatl.

The pre-Columbians

The pre-Columbian empires flourished in Central America, where they included the Aztecs and Mayas, and on the high plateaus of the Andes mountains, with the Incas.

s of the Book

The three religions of

Judaism, Christianity, and Islam are the three major monotheist religions of the present day. They share a belief in one God, whose word was revealed to humankind and then written in a book.

◑ **apostle** (from the Greek *apostolos*, "one who is sent out"): name given to the twelve companions or disciples whom Jesus Christ chose to spread his word across the world (and also used of St. Paul).

◑ **Christian:** a person who believes Jesus Christ to be the Son of God.

◑ **commandment:** rule or law that must be followed. Moses received from God the Ten Commandments that he passed on to the Hebrews.

◑ **faith:** belief.

◑ **Hebrews:** people of the ancient East whose history is recounted in the Bible. The Hebrews were the ancestors of the Jews.

◑ **Jew:** a person belonging to the religious and cultural community based on Jewish law and practice.

◑ **monotheist:** person who believes in only one God.

◑ **Muslim:** a follower of Islam.

◑ **patriarch:** in the Bible, a head of a family or tribe who lived to a great age.

◑ **prophet:** someone who has been called by God, who listens to his calling and who transmits it to others by words and deeds.

◑ **revelation** (of God): manifestation of God to humankind to make them aware of his existence.

◑ **sacrifice:** killing a living creature as an offering to a god.

The three **monotheist** religions appeared at different periods in the ancient Middle East: Judaism through Abraham, Isaac, and Jacob, in the 19th century B.C. in the land of Canaan; Christianity, taught by Jesus Christ and the twelve **apostles**, in the 1st century of the Christian era, in Judaea and Galilee; and Islam inspired by Mohammed (Muhammed), in A.D. 622 in Arabia.

The Bible, the Gospel, the Koran

These three religions see it as their role to make known the one God. They teach that he speaks through prophets, wise men, and sometimes messengers (angels). The word of God is written down in holy books: for the Jews, the Bible (Torah); for Christians, the Bible complemented by the Gospels; and for Muslims, the Koran. The Bible is the story of the life and hopes of Hebrew people. It is also the account of the revelation of the one God who made himself known by revealing his name (Yahweh, "I am") and by giving his **commandments**. The first person who believed in the **revelation** of the one God was Abraham.

Abraham prepares to sacrifice his son, from the Beit Alpha synagogue, Israel, 6th century A.D.

e Book

representation of Jesus and Mohammed visiting the prophet Isaiah

The patriarch Abraham

According to the Bible, around the 19th century B.C. in Ur in Mesopotamia Abraham heard the word of God: "Leave your country and go to the country that I will give you." Obeying the divine word, he leaves for the land of Canaan, which is to be called the land of Israel. There, God makes a covenant with Abraham and promises him innumerable descendants because he has believed in God. The Koran describes how Abraham leaves Babylon for Syria-Palestine. Today, Jews, Christians, and Muslims all are in one respect inheritors of Abraham, for like him they have **faith** in one God.

The test of faith in the Bible

The best-known episode of Abraham's life, as told in the Bible, is the sacrifice of Isaac. The patriarch's first son, Ishmael, was born to his servant Hagar. His wife Sara had borne no children, but then God grants the old couple a son, Isaac. God puts Abraham to the test by asking him to sacrifice this son. Abraham does not hesitate, but God stays his arm when he is poised to kill Isaac and replaces the victim by a ram. Several meanings are given to this episode (for example, at this time when humans were sacrificed to gods, it shows that God forbids such killings). However, all interpretations agree that it makes Abraham the exemplary man who has faith in God above all else: this is why he is called the "father of believers."

The interpretation of this test

The story of Abraham and Isaac has specific and quite different meanings in each of the three monotheist religions. For the Jews, it was a divine test, which took place on Mount Moryah, traditionally situated in Jerusalem, where King Solomon would build the Temple of God, the place of his divine presence. For Christians, the sacrifice of Isaac presages that of Jesus, who will die on the cross to save all people. For Muslims, the victim is Ishmael (considered the ancestor of the Arab people and thus of the Muslims). His brother Isaac is born as recompense for this sacrifice. Many think the sacrifice took place in Arabia on the road to Mecca, where Ibrahim (Abraham) had come to worship God. These different interpretations have caused debates throughout history.

The name of God

Although the followers of the three religions worshiped one God, they gave him different names. Among Jews, his name is four letters, which, in respect, are never said: YHWH (written Yahweh by adding vowels, but when read aloud, it is replaced by Adonai, the Lord). Among Christians, he is God, the Father, the Son, and the Holy Spirit. For Muslims, he is Allah. For all of them he is the Merciful One. His name—in all its forms—signifies that he is the source of all existence. ☐

Adam and Eve

The three religions of the Book recognize Adam and Eve as the ancestors of humanity. They lived in an ideal garden, the Earthly Paradise (above). One day, a serpent, the symbol of evil, encouraged them to eat a forbidden fruit. Adam and Eve yielded to temptation and bit into the apple offered by the serpent. As punishment, God then banished them from Paradise (below).

Judaism

Judaism is the religion of the Jewish people. It is also their history, culture, and way of life. It was the first religion to affirm the existence of a single God.

- **circumcision:** operation that consists in cutting away the fold of skin covering the glans of the penis.
- **diaspora:** a Greek word that means "dispersion." The Diaspora refers to the dispersion of the Jews from Palestine, and now those Jews living outside the state of Israel.
- **ghetto:** in a city, a separate district where Jews were forced to live.
- **Israel:** the name given to Jacob, Abraham's grandson, and then to all the Jewish people, referred to as Israel, the people of Israel, or Israelites. It is also the name given to the state established in the Near East in 1948, the state of Israel.
- **profession of faith:** solemn proclamation that commits a person's or a community's faith.
- **prophet:** someone who has been called by God, who listens to his calling and who transmits it by words, deeds, and at times silences.
- **synagogue** (from the Greek *sunagoge* meaning "meeting"): a building where Jewish worship is celebrated.

Moses receiving the Tablets of the Law

For nearly 2,000 years following the biblical era, the Jewish people lived scattered throughout the different countries of the world, united by their faith and their hope for better times for themselves and for all humanity.

Abraham, Isaac, and Jacob

The story of the Hebrews as told in the Bible begins when Abraham leaves Ur in Chaldea (present-day Iraq) for the land of Canaan, which God promises to give to his descendants. Abraham undertakes to obey the one God and makes a covenant with him, which is symbolized by **circumcision**. Abraham's faith grows through the tests to which God puts him, such as that of the sacrifice of his son Isaac. Jacob, son of Isaac,

receives the name of Israel. The descendants of Abraham are then forced by famine to seek refuge in Egypt where they are kept in slavery for four centuries.

Moses

God chose Moses to bring the Hebrews out of Egypt—an event commemorated by Passover—and to lead them through the desert to the Promised Land of Canaan. On Mount Sinai, Moses receives from God the Ten Commandments or the Decalogue (Ten Words), which are to be engraved on two stone tablets, the Tablets of the Law, and carried in a coffer, the Ark of the Covenant. All the Hebrews, the children of Israel, enter into the covenant by accepting the Ten Commandments. For 40 years, they survive journeying in the desert thanks to divine protection. Led by Joshua, Moses' successor, they embark on the conquest of the Promised Land.

The kings and prophets

At the end of the second millennium B.C., the Hebrews decided to have a king. The prophet Samuel chose Saul and, later, David (1015–975 B.C.), who makes Jerusalem the capital of the kingdom. David's son, Solomon, builds a temple to house the Ark of the Covenant in Jerusalem, which is to be the center of the religious life of Israel. The kingdom is then divided, with Israel in the north and Judah in the south. This is the period of the **prophets** who, often simple shepherds or farmers inspired by God, urge the princes and the people to respect the commandments.

The exile to Babylon and the return

The kingdom of Israel was unable to resist invaders, who conquer it in 722 B.C. In

the menorah being carried off to Rome after the destruction of the Temple

587 B.C., Nebuchadnezzar, king of Babylon, invaded the kingdom of Judah, destroyed the Temple and deported most of Judah's inhabitants (henceforth known as Jews) to Babylon. Around 538 B.C., the Jews returned to Judah, rebuilt the Temple, and reconstituted their religious life. Soon afterwards, the Greeks and then the Romans occupied the country.

The Diaspora

In A.D. 70, following a rebellion by the Jews, the Romans burned Jerusalem. The only part of the Temple to survive is the Western Wall or Wailing Wall. Many Jews left for Egypt, Northern Africa, Europe, and Babylonia. The history of the **Diaspora** is marked by persecutions suffered by European Jews during the Middle Ages. Often forced to live

in special areas or ghettos, Jews were expelled from England in 1290, from France in 1394, and from Spain in 1492. During all this time they continued to deepen their religious culture. At the end of the 19th century, there was an increase in anti-Semitism, which preached hatred of Jews. In tsarist Russia, Jews fled from pogroms (massacres). During the Second World War, around six million Jews (men, women, and children) were methodically exterminated by the German Nazis. Known as the Holocaust, this was the most terrible anti-Jewish persecution in history, carried out in Germany and in all the Nazi-occupied countries of Europe. Today more than four million Jews live in the state of Israel, which was founded in 1948. Nearly 6 million Jews live in the United States and there are roughly 4.5 million Jews in Europe.

The menorah

The menorah was the seven-branched golden candle holder that always burned in the Temple of Solomon. It was carried off by the Romans after the destruction of the Temple in A.D. 70. To Jews, it symbolizes the lost Temple.

The migrations of the Hebrews

It is thought that on leaving Ur, Abraham followed caravan routes across the desert. In the flight from Egypt, Moses and the Hebrews probably skirted the Promised Land before entering it from the east.

—— Abraham's route
—— Moses' route

Mount Sinai, where Moses received the Ten Commandments

A rabbi sounds the shofar, or ram's horn

The Bible, the Talmud, and their message

Jar containing the Dead Sea Scrolls

In 1948, jars containing scrolls were found in caves near the Dead Sea. Some of these scrolls contained passages of the Bible written in Hebrew and Aramaic, a language spoken in the Near East in ancient times. They date from the 2nd century B.C. and are the oldest biblical manuscripts known, closest to the period when the Bible was written down. It is thought that the Hebrew Bible (the part Christians call the Old Testament) was written, in Hebrew and Aramaic, between the 13th and 3rd centuries B.C. Until this discovery, the oldest surviving texts were written in Greek, based on a translation from Hebrew. Today, the Bible is translated into 1,435 languages and is read by hundreds of millions of people.

The Jewish religion rests on a book, the Bible, and on other writings that comment on it, including the Talmud. The Bible affirms the existence of one God who has made a covenant with the people of Israel.

The Bible

The Bible (from the Greek *biblos*, "book") is the basis of all Jewish thought. It is made up of twenty-four books written in Hebrew, in three section, the Torah, the Nebiim, and the Kethubim. The Torah is an instruction or a way to follow, which is the meaning of the word in Hebrew. The Torah is made up of five books known as the Pentateuch (Greek for "five books"): Genesis, Exodus, Leviticus, Numbers, and Deuteronomy. Here are listed the account of the creation of the world, the founding events of Israel (God's covenant with Abraham), then the adventure of the

people of Israel under the leadership of Moses. However, the Torah is more than a story and more than a body of law, with numerous instructions centered on the Ten Commandments and the precepts of love for God and for one's neighbor. The Torah is the most fundamental part of the Bible. It is read in synagogues, in Hebrew, each morning of the Sabbath and on festivals from a parchment roll on which it has been copied by hand.

In the Nebiim or Prophets, the early prophets and the later prophets are distinguished. The early prophets recount the history of Israel from the conquest of Canaan to the destruction of the first Temple of Jerusalem. Their account, directly inspired by God, shows that the divine presence has

the rolls of the Torah in front of the Western Wall or Wailing Wall in Jerusalem

reading the Torah in a synagogue

manifested itself throughout history. The later prophets include three major prophets (Isaiah, Jeremiah, and Ezekiel) and twelve minor prophets (including Amos and Jonah) who emphasize the moral content of the divine message. Their words, like all the Bible, are intended first for Israel, but also through Israel for all humanity. The Kethubim, or Writings, vary greatly: psalms, proverbs, historical accounts, and reflections on the problems of life, death, and suffering. The Bible is also known as the "written Torah."

The Talmud

Talmud means "teaching." The Bible is a living message, and learned men were—and still are—responsible for interpreting what is written in it. In the Talmud, they drew up precise laws that make it possible to apply the Bible's commandments to each circumstance of life. These oral teachings were later written down and now constitute an encyclopedia of Jewish law and thought.

The unity of God

"God is one." This is the fundamental affirmation of the Bible and of Judaism, proclaimed in the passage of the Torah called *Shema Israel*. This is also the Jewish profession of faith, which Jews recite at dawn and dusk every day of their life. God revealed himself to Moses under the name formed of the four Hebrew letters YHWH (Yahweh), which means "the one who is, who was, and who will be." In prayer, this name is pronounced as "Adonai," which translates as *lord* or *eternal*. God is the creator of the world, the merciful and just God who intervenes in history. He has "brought Israel out of the slavery of Egypt," which shows that he is close to the most downtrodden.

an illuminated Hebrew manuscript

The covenant and the election

God gave the Torah so that, by obeying it, Israel should become "a people of priests and a holy nation." Israel was chosen to bear witness to the love of the creator for all of humanity. The covenant is a responsibility, not a privilege.

The Messiah and messianism

For Jews, to believe in the coming of the messiah is to hope that a day will come when peace, justice, and fraternity will prevail in all nations. The people of Israel will then be reunited in the land of their ancestors and their trials will be over. So it is necessary to live according to the Torah, and God will send a man, the messiah, "filled with the spirit of wisdom, of love and fear of God. . . ." ☐

The holy ark in the synagogue

The synagogue (in Hebrew, bet ha-knesset) is the meeting place of the Jewish community for public prayer and study. It is built so that the congregation faces toward Jerusalem, where the Temple stood before its destruction. Only two or three pieces of furniture are involved in worship. The principal one is the holy ark (see below) that holds the rolls of the Torah and in front of which burns a perpetual lamp. There is also a raised pulpit on which the Torah is placed and from which its texts are read aloud. In front of this pulpit, a lower table is used by the member of the community who leads the service.

The festival of Pesach (Passover)

Practices and festivals

Reading the Torah

At his bar mitzvah (Hebrew words meaning that the boy becomes a "son of the commandment"), the child reads the Torah in the synagogue in the presence of his parents and all the members of the community. He is then considered an adult. This moment is the climax of years of study of the Torah, involving the learning of Hebrew.

A Jewish believer must obey the commandments of the Torah. From the Torah verse, "You shall love your neighbor as yourself," derive the rules of conduct toward others.

Blessing, prayer, and study

For the Jewish believer, every happiness that life has brought him is a gift from God, so he blesses all the actions that he carries out. Three daily prayers, in the morning, the afternoon, and the evening, punctuate his day. In the mornings and the evenings, he recites the *Shema Israel* ("Hear, Israel . . ."). In the morning, he puts on a prayer shawl (the tallith), a symbol of the divine presence, and wears on his forehead small cases of leather (tefillin) containing four passages of the Torah, to symbolize his attachment to God and his commandments. Study and teaching of the sacred texts are obligatory.

The synagogue and the home

Jewish believers practice their religion both in the synagogue and at home. The synagogue is the place of prayer and study. The religious guide is the rabbi, who teaches, oversees ceremonies, and advises the faithful. Fixed to the entrance of the house is the mezuzah, a small case in which verses of the Torah including the *Shema* are written. The believer observes a number of rules concerning food, called *kashrut*. These rules include a distinction between pure and impure animals. Only cloven-hoofed ruminants, aquatic animals with scales and fins, and poultry are permitted as food. Pigs, horses, rabbits, eels, oysters, mussels, and other seafoods are forbidden. There are other such rules, the purpose of which is to sanctify everyday life.

Stages of life

Circumcision (*Berith Milah*) of boys at the age of eight days is the sign of God's covenant with Israel. Religious maturity—*bar mitzvah* for boys at age 13 and *bat mitzvah* for girls at 12—confirms the years of study of the Torah. Marriage takes place in the synagogue or at home. After death and prayers for the dead, relatives and friends go to the house of the deceased to pray for seven days. They recite the *Kaddish*, a prayer calling for the coming of the kingdom of God.

The Sabbath

This is the seventh day of the week, beginning on Friday evening and lasting until Saturday evening. It is the day of rest, observed in memory of the creation of the world, which was completed by God on the seventh day, and in memory of the flight from Egypt, when God gave freedom to his people. All work is forbidden (such as

Celebrating a bar mitzvah

a young boy wearing tefillin (or phylacteries) on his forehead and around his arms

person asks pardon from his neighbor for faults committed, comes Yom Kippur, the Day of Atonement. This is the most solemn day of the year and is marked by a day of fasting given over to prayer in the synagogue. The day ends with the sounding of the shofar. Five days later, Sukkoth, the festival of tabernacles, lasts a week. In memory of the wanderings of the Jews led by Moses in the desert, each family builds a hut roofed with branches, where they eat a symbolic meal. The eighth day is the festival of the Torah, Simchat Torah. In December, the festival of lights, Hanukkah, commemorates the victory of Judas Maccabeus over the Greeks in 167 B.C. Purim (February-March) is a popular festival, which recalls that Esther, when she became queen of Persia, saved her people from extermination. As a sign of gratitude, sweets are exchanged and gifts presented to the poor. In spring, Pesach (Passover) commemorates the flight from Egypt. This festival is celebrated at home in a ceremony called the Seder. During a meal, psalms are sung and passages from the Bible are read. Symbolic foods and drink—are taken: unleavened bread, bitter herbs, salt water, and four glasses of wine. Fifty days later, Shavuoth (Pentecost) commemorates the gift of the Torah to Moses; in the synagogue, the Ten Commandments are read out.
□

Marriage ceremony

During the celebration, the couple remains under the huppah or wedding canopy, which is a symbol of the home they are to create. The rabbi reads the ketubah, the marriage contract, in the presence of the parents and witnesses. After the nuptial blessings, the bridegroom breaks a glass in memory of the destruction of the Temple.

lighting a fire or writing letters), for this day must be consecrated to the Lord by prayer in the synagogue, reading and study of the Torah, and also by visiting the sick.

Festivals

The Jewish calendar begins at the symbolic date of the creation of the world (1998 was the year 5758). Rosh Hashanah is the new year, which is celebrated in September-October. In the synagogues, the shofar, or ram's horn, is blown, recalling Abraham's sacrifice and his faith in God. At home apples and honey are eaten, symbolizing the desire for a pleasant year. After ten days dedicated to prayer and repentance, during which each

a Jew wearing the tallith or prayer shawl

Our era dates from the birth of Jesus. According to his disciples, he is the Messiah (or Christ), the Son of God who gave his life to save humanity and who was raised from the dead. Christianity is founded on this belief.

Christianity

- **doctrine:** for Christians, a body of beliefs, ideas, and rules defining a concept of someone in relation to God, to the world, and to other people.
- **dogma:** fundamental principle considered to be an indisputable truth of a religious doctrine.
- **heretic:** a person who denies a dogma or rejects aspects of the official doctrine.
- **liturgy:** the body of rules regulating worship, such as the progress of a service, choice of prayers, and so on.
- **messiah:** God's envoy sent to Earth to introduce an era of justice.
- **miracle:** inexplicable phenomenon attributed to God's intervention.
- **monasticism:** condition of, or life as, a monk. Monks and nuns obey the same rule of life or monastic rule.
- **New Testament:** the Christian Bible contains the Old Testament, corresponding to the Hebrew Bible, and the New Testament, which contains the four Gospels, the Acts of the Apostles, the Letters or Epistles (mainly the Letters of St. Paul), and the Revelation of St. John.
- **schism:** a break in the unity of a religious community or church.

Christianity appeared in the land of Israel during the time of its occupation by the Romans. A Jew of Nazareth, Jesus was acknowledged by his followers as the **Messiah** announced by the Bible and as the Son of God. He said that he was sent to extend to all humanity the covenant made between Yahweh and the Jewish people. God, who in the Old Testament had spoken through the prophets, now spoke through his son Jesus Christ. Faith in Jesus is what separates Christians from Jews, who are still awaiting the Messiah. Jesus' life and teachings are known through the texts which, for Christians, form the second part of the Bible, the **New Testament**.

The life of Jesus
The life of Christ is recounted in four small books called the Gospels (meaning "good

the crucifixion of Christ on Mount Golgotha, in Jerusalem

The Last Supper, Jesus' last meal with his disciples

the birth of Jesus

news"), written between A.D. 65 and 100 by Matthew, Mark, Luke, and John. According to Luke's account, the Angel of God announces to Mary, who is betrothed to Joseph, that by the intervention of the Holy Spirit she will have a child who will be the Son of God. Jesus is born in Bethlehem and grows up in Nazareth. When he is around 30 years old, he is baptized by John the Baptist. He then chooses twelve apostles: Peter, Andrew, James the Great, John, Philip, Bartholomew, Matthew, Thomas, James the Less, Simon, Jude (or Thaddeus), and Judas. For three years, the apostles travel the country with Jesus, proclaiming the good news. Jesus befriends the outcast and the poor; his message, sometimes accompanied by miracles, is accepted with enthusiasm by the multitudes. However, he offends the religious authorities and political powers. In A.D. 30, he is arrested during Passover, brought before the Sanhedrin (Jewish court), and then delivered to the Roman governor, Pontius Pilate. He is condemned to die on

the cross, like a slave, and is buried. Three days later, his tomb is found to be empty. The apostles then claim that they have seen Jesus resurrected, that is, returned to life, and that he remained for forty days among them, before "ascending to heaven." Before leaving them, Jesus promises the coming of the Holy Spirit and sends his apostles to proclaim the Gospel to all nations.

The message of Jesus Christ

Christ's message is that God is love, that he is a father for all men, and that he loves them so much that he gave them his son, who sacrificed himself—accepting to die so that men may be saved, in other words, that they may have eternal life after death. He calls each person to "love his neighbor like himself," as he, Jesus, has loved humanity. □

the resurrection of Jesus

The chrismon

A symbol of Christianity, the chrismon is formed by the first letters of the word *Christ* in Greek: XP—the X (chi) corresponds to "ch" and P (rhō) to "r."

The good shepherd

Jesus frequently compared himself to a shepherd (pastor) who watches over not only his flock (the faithful) but also lost sheep. The first Christians often represented Jesus in the form of a shepherd. The lamb, associated with purity and innocence, is another symbol of Christ.

a 9th-century mosaic depicting angels

The Church during the first millennium

The first Christians and the catacombs

The catacombs are underground cemeteries and, contrary to what was long believed, have never been used for secret ceremonies. The first Christians met there at the tombs of the martyrs (a Greek word meaning "witness"), the name given to Christians who died rather than renounce their religion. By honoring the one true God, they did not worship the Roman emperor and so were tortured and put to death. Some emperors had them crucified or thrown to the wild animals in the arena. By accepting such suffering, these Christians bore witness to their faith.

the pope and the emperor presiding over a council in the 8th century

The Church (from the Greek *kurikon*, meaning "the Lord's [house]") of the first Christians was founded in Jerusalem as a community around the apostles. After Pentecost, the sending of the Spirit announced by Jesus, the apostles went out to proclaim the good news of the resurrection of Christ. They founded churches across the Mediterranean world, in Asia Minor, in Greece, in Rome itself, and probably in Arabia and Syria.

The spread of Christianity

The apostle Paul (born about A.D. 15—died about A.D. 67) affirmed that it was not necessary to be Jewish to become a Christian. Around the year 48, the followers of the new religion stopped practicing the rites of Judaism and were then excluded from the Jewish community. It was in Antioch, in Syria, that they were referred to for the first time as Christians. The emerging religion was introduced to everyone, in accordance with the words of Jesus: "Make disciples of all nations." Following those at Jerusalem, Constantinople, Rome, Antioch, and Alexandria, other Christian communities developed along the trade routes of the Mediterranean basin. Emperor Constantine gave Christians freedom to worship in 313, and Christianity became the official religion of the Roman empire in 393 under the emperor Theodosius.

the baptism of Christ

The first councils of the Church

Bishops led the Christian communities and met in councils. At these assemblies each bishop reported on what he did in his province, and almost all would agree on decisions that would be universal. Seven great councils (Jerusalem, Nicaea I and II, Constantinople I and II, Ephesus, and Chalcedon) set down the faith of the Church in a text called the *credo* (Latin for "I believe"), or creed. This text is what must be accepted to become Christian. The council also defined fundamental truths called **dogmas**. Those who rejected these dogmas or tried to modify them were known as **heretics**, that is, "those who make a mistaken choice." They were excluded from the community and persecuted. From this time, Christians began to venerate saints—people who led an exemplary life in accordance with the will of God. Unique authority was acknowledged in the bishop of Rome, because his Church had been founded by the apostles Peter and Paul and because he was regarded as Peter's successor.

The first monks

From the 4th century A.D., monks went out into the deserts of Egypt and Syria to live a life of poverty, prayer, and work. From these first monks arose the great Christian movement of **monasticism**, in the East under St. Basil (329–379) and in the West under St. Benedict (about 480–547).

Christian festivals

Each year, festivals commemorate the major events of the life of Jesus Christ. Although some are derived from Judaism, Christians have given them new meaning. The festival of Christmas celebrates the birth of Jesus Christ. Epiphany recalls the adoration of the Magi, the Three Wise Men who came from the East to render homage to Jesus just after his birth. Preceded by the 40 days of fasting and privation known as Lent, Easter is the most important festival, since it celebrates the resurrection of Christ. Ascension, forty days after Easter, celebrates Christ's ascent to heaven. Then, ten days after Ascension, Pentecost commemorates the day when the Holy Spirit came down on the assembled apostles, making them capable of being understood in every language, so they could spread the Christian faith.

The sacraments

The sacraments are visible signs, the outward actions that admit a Christian to the spiritual life. The principal sacraments are:
– baptism, which introduces new believers to the Church;
– confirmation, during which the Holy Spirit penetrates the soul of the Christian, as at Pentecost;
– the eucharist or communion, the most important moment in Christian worship, when they receive the body and blood of Christ in the form of bread and wine;
– the sacrament of reconciliation (or confession), which grants the Church's pardon to persons who repent of their sins;
– marriage;
– ordination, which gives priests the power to celebrate the sacraments; and
– anointing of the sick, which prepares the Christian for death. ☐

The symbol of the fish

The first Christians chose the image of the fish to symbolize Jesus Christ. "Jesus Christ, Son of God, saviour" is written in Greek as Iesous Christos Theou Uios Soter. The initials of these words form *ichthus*, which means "fish" in Greek.

Communion

Communion is the sacrament by which Christians reenact the sacrifice of Christ. Communion is taken either standing or kneeling.

crusaders sack Constantinople in 1204

Expansion and division of the Church

The Inquisition

The Inquisition was a Church court set up in 1229 to seek out and try heretics (those who did not observe official doctrine). It was overseen by the monks of the order of St. Dominic, seen here burning books that did not conform to the Catholic faith.

In the 5th century, barbarians divided up the western part of the Roman empire, which collapsed in 476. They founded rival kingdoms governed by warring kings. Christianity was the only link uniting them; all Christian kings respected the authority of the Church of Rome. The language used in the West was Latin. By contrast, the empire in the East maintained a form of unity until 1453. It was known as the Byzantine Empire, because its capital, Constantinople, was formerly named Byzantium. The language of the empire was Greek, and within its borders a brilliant Christian culture flourished around the Mediterranean, rivalled after 650 by Islam.

In the East, the Orthodox Church

Different political development over such a long time led to the **schism** (separation), which was to divide the Church. In 1054, a quarrel broke out between the pope in Rome, Leo IX, and the patriarch of Constantinople, Michael Cerularius. The break was made definitive after the sack of Constantinople during the fourth crusade in 1204. On one side stood the Church that was "orthodox" ("which kept to the true **doctrine**" of the seven councils), rejected amendments to the text of the credo made by the Western Church, and did not recognize the universal authority of the pope. On the other side was the Church that was "Roman Catholic" ("which maintains the world's unity"), in which the pope played an increasingly central role. It was not until 1964 that Pope Paul VI and Patriarch Athenagoras reestablished dialogue between the Catholic and Orthodox churches.

In the West, the Catholic Church

In the 12th and 13th centuries, a religious civilization flourished in western Europe. The Church of Rome exercised authority through the priests and monks who formed the clergy. This hierarchical system directed the faithful and administered hospitals and universities. The first university was founded around 1110 at Bologna in Italy, followed by Paris, Cologne, Oxford, and others. Students came from all over Europe to study with renowned teachers, all of whom were clerics. Romanesque abbeys and, later, Gothic cathedrals were built throughout the Christian world. In the 12th century, St. Bernard founded the Cistercian order of monks. During this period the crusades also began. These were military expeditions intended to reconquer the holy city of Jerusalem, which was then in the hands of the Muslims.

In the 13th century, orders of mendicant

This richly decorated bishop's staff testifies to the power of the Church in the 13th century.

monks were established: the Dominicans, founded by St. Dominic, and the Franciscans, founded by St. Francis of Assisi. Alongside this spiritual flowering, other actions tarnished the Church's image: the Jews were persecuted; the crusades involved pillaging and massacres; and the courts of the Inquisition used torture to obtain confessions

Martin Luther (in the foreground) and Protestant thinkers

and passed harsh sentences against heretics.

Birth of Protestantism

At the end of the 15th century, scholars known as humanists began to question the nature and teaching of the biblical texts and the role and conduct of the Church. They demanded that the Church be reformed. In Germany, Martin Luther (1483–1546) denounced a number of abuses and posed a series of questions that were fundamental to faith. The Church expelled him by excommunication. Luther's protest started the Reformation, a movement whose supporters came to be known as "Protestants" and who diverged into various strands. From Germany, the movement spread to Scandinavia, Switzerland, France, the Low Countries, and Scotland. In England, Henry VIII proclaimed himself head of the Church of England (or Anglican Church). In the 1500s and 1600s, Europe was torn apart by religious wars fought between Catholics and Protestants. The Catholic Church embarked on a Counterreformation. New orders of teachers and missionaries, such as the Jesuits, were created to defend Catholicism.

Ecumenicism

It was not until the 1960s that the separate Christian churches started a dialogue for reconciliation, known as the ecumenical movement. Started by the Protestant churches, in this movement church leaders and ordinary believers met to try to find ways to regain lost unity. ☐

John Calvin (1509–1564)

Calvin was born in Noyon, France. He studied Latin,

Greek, and Hebrew, but in 1533 he converted to the ideas of Luther. He had to leave France to escape the Inquisition and preached the Reformation. Taking refuge in Switzerland, he reformed Geneva, which he made into a model city where strict religious morals prevailed and where games of cards, novels, and dancing were prohibited. In 1535 he published his *Institutes of the Christian Religion*. Like Luther, Calvin believed that the Bible alone had authority in religious matters. However, he also believed in predestination. His thinking was that because of sin human nature is evil. God alone decides to save certain people and to give them eternal life. All the good a person may do cannot change this. Calvin's thought is the basis of Calvinism.

Orthodox Christian religious ceremony

The Orthodox Christians

Icon of the Trinity

Icons are painted according to precise rules on a background (usually gilded) that has no light or shadow. Represented here are the three persons of the Trinity (the Father, the Son, and the Holy Spirit), which for Christians are contained in one God. Icons can also represent saints.

Virgin with Child

For Orthodox Christians and for Catholics, the Virgin Mary is the "Mother of God" and of men, because Christ on the cross said to John: "Son, behold your mother."

Orthodox Christians, those who maintain the "right doctrine," number around 170 million. They insist on continuity with the Church of early Christianity, the Church of the martyrs, and of the seven great councils of bishops that formulated the faith. The text of the creed, which is the foundation of the Christian faith, is not exactly the same for Orthodox Christians and Catholics.

Orthodox Christians do not acknowledge the universal authority of the pope, the supreme head of the Catholic Church. The Orthodox faith emphasizes the action of the Holy Spirit (the third person of the Trinity) whose force penetrates not only the soul of the believer, but also the very substance of his body, and from there, the substance of the world.

Ritual and festivals

The Orthodox Church celebrates certain festivals with special emphasis, including Epiphany, Easter, and the Transfiguration (an episode of Christ's life when God made himself heard). The Eastern churches have kept the Julian calendar, based on the phases of the moon, while the Church of Rome and other Western churches adopted the Gregorian calendar, as reformed by Pope Gregory XIII in 1582. This is why the dates of the Orthodox and Catholic festivals differ. The sacraments of baptism, in which the believer is totally immersed in water; confirmation; and communion are received together. Through these it is possible to participate in the solemn ceremony of the Mystery of Mysteries, the eucharist or communion in the Body and Blood of Christ. This sacrament (Orthodox Christians prefer the word *mystery*) is administered in the double form of bread and wine.

Liturgy and icons

The central event of the liturgical year is Easter, the "festival of festivals," which is followed by forty days during which the usual forms of greeting are replaced by the joyful exclamation, "Christ is risen!," to which the response is, "In truth, he is risen." Orthodox religious ceremonies are long. Their purpose is to awaken the heart of the believer to the beauty of God through chants, prostrations, the glow of candles, perfume of incense, splendor of icons, and richness of adornments. Icons play an important role in the **liturgy**. The word comes from the Greek *eikôn*, "image."

Orthodox priest

a festival in honor of St. Sergius of Radonezh, a Russian saint

women praying before an iconostasis

Believers kiss the icons and light candles before them. Icons are also a way of teaching through pictures on the walls of the church, on the iconostasis (a screen in Orthodox Churches separating the congregation from the altar), and in homes, where they are a call to prayer. Ordinary people recite a simple prayer, in which the name of Jesus is whispered; it is known as the "prayer of the heart."

The various Orthodox churches

The Orthodox community is divided into several churches that have links with each other but that have their own leader or patriarch. The oldest churches derive from the eastern patriarchates of the Roman empire: Antioch, Alexandria, Jerusalem, and Constantinople. The other churches

administer themselves and usually correspond to a country: these are the churches of Russia (the largest in number), Romania, Serbia, Greece, Bulgaria, Cyprus, and the United States. The Orthodox Christians scattered across the world depend both directly on these churches and on other communities, including the churches of Finland, of Crete, and of Africa.

The organization of Orthodox Churches

Monastic life plays a key role in the Orthodox world. Mount Athos in the north of Greece is the largest monastery in Christendom. Since the 6th century, bishops, who remain celibate, have been chosen from among monks. Orthodox priests are permitted to marry. □

The Oriental Christians

Some Christian churches adopted rites and even beliefs different from those of the majority of Christians. While some of these churches later joined the Catholic or the Orthodox churches, others remained independent. Among the latter, the largest is the Ethiopian Church, which

has 14 million followers. Above, an Ethiopian priest is shown. Although this church in Africa had no contact with other Christian communities over several centuries, it kept its faith. However, its practices developed in a unique way, and because of the presence of a large Jewish minority, its rituals are much influenced by Judaism.

reading from the Bible during worship

The Protestants

Barbara Harris

In 1980, Barbara Harris was consecrated as a bishop of the Episcopal Church of the United States. Most reformed churches accepted women as pastors. The Church of England accepted women as priests in 1992.

The Anglican Church

Queen Elizabeth II (above) is head of the Church of England. Its first head was King Henry VIII (1491–1547). The queen appoints bishops in agreement with the Archbishop of Canterbury.

Protestantism began in the 16th century in Europe with the Reformation started by Martin Luther (see p. 45). Protestantism now has almost 400 million followers and has become very diverse. It includes many churches and movements, united by the key tenets, God alone, Scripture alone, and Grace alone. God alone: Protestants believe that only faith in Jesus Christ can bring salvation, that is, eternal life. Scripture alone: For Protestants, God makes himself known to each believer through the Bible, without the intermediary of priests or Church. This is why, within Protestantism, there are many tendencies, based on different ways of reading the Bible. Grace alone: The

benevolent will of God is known as Grace. It is only by his will that God gives persons the faith that saves them and wins eternal life. This means that a person is saved not by good actions but only by the intervention of divine grace. Unlike the Catholic and Orthodox churches, the Protestant churches have little dogma and a less hierarchical organization.

The church and worship

Believers go to their church for worship on Sunday and to celebrate the major events of life. The church is a meeting place and a place for prayer. There are fewer statues and pictures, the

two women pastors

48

the interior of a Protestant church

sole decoration often being a bare cross. A pulpit, from which the Bible is read and commented on during a sermon, is the focal point of the service. The rites are sober and sometimes reduced to essentials. But the singing of hymns encourages the congregation to join fully in worship. Protestants consider God alone to be the object of prayer and veneration. Therefore, most do not practice any cult of the saints or the Virgin Mary. Three principal festivals are celebrated: Christmas, Easter, and Pentecost (see p. 43).

The sacraments and piety

Protestants recognize only the two sacraments mentioned in the Gospels. These are baptism (which is not compulsory at birth), the symbol of the covenant with God; and the Lord's Supper (or eucharist), the commemoration of Christ's last meal with the disciples, during which believers take communion. Protestantism encourages collective and family piety centered on study of the Bible. Apart from the religious education received within their family, children may attend Bible school or Sunday school, where they study the Old and New Testaments.

The role of the pastor

For Protestants, no intermediary is required between God and the individual. The role of the Protestant clergy—such as a pastor, for example—therefore differs from that of a Catholic priest. The pastor is a believer who, like all other church members who are adequately prepared, teaches the biblical message and administers the sacraments, the signs of Grace. However, the religious studies that he has undertaken make him better able to guide the faithful. The original meaning of the word *pastor* is "guide of the flock." A pastor may be married, and a woman may become a pastor.

The organization of Protestant churches

Some Protestant churches are organized in parishes or other small groups, directed by the pastor or minister, and a group of elected elders (church members). Each parish delegates representatives to the regional synod, a church assembly. Each regional synod sends delegates to the national synod, at which the important decisions of the denomination are made.

The principal components of Protestantism

Protestantism is made up of:
– Churches that have their own rules and methods of organization. The most important are Lutheran (70 million followers), Calvinist (Reformed or Presbyterian Churches, 55 million followers), and Episcopalian or Anglican (more than 60 million followers in England and across the world). Mennonites, Baptists, Methodists, Quakers, Adventists, and Pentecostals are other Protestant groups that have evolved, especially in the United States.
– movements to help the deprived in society, such as the Salvation Army.

The World Council of Churches was founded by Protestants in 1948. This organization brings together, in Geneva, the great majority of Protestant and Orthodox churches (about 300 churches and 500 million Christians). ☐

Martin Luther King

Son of a black American Baptist pastor, he was born in 1929 in Atlanta, Georgia, a southern state of the United States where racism was strong. He was a good student who dreamed of becoming a lawyer to defend blacks. After going to college at the age of 15, he decided at the age of

17 to become a pastor. He founded the Southern Christian Leadership Conference in which blacks and whites, united by the same Christian ideal, campaigned in nonviolent ways for equality. He asked the citizens of Montgomery, Alabama, to boycott the city's segregated buses, in which different seats were allocated for whites and blacks. He was imprisoned several times but won the support of President Kennedy. He was assassinated in 1968.

mass celebrated by several priests

The Catholics

The Virgin of Czestochowa

Pilgrimages to the Black Virgin of Czestochowa in Poland attract millions of Catholics.

Confession

According to the Gospel, the apostles received the power to pardon sins in the name of God. Below, a child confesses his sins to a priest who will give him absolution, or pardon him. Nowadays, Catholics prefer to use the term *reconciliation* rather than *confession*.

In its current usage, the word *Catholic* describes the part of the Church that since the 16th century has recognized the universal authority of the pope, whose seat is in Rome. With more than one billion followers spread over more than 40 nations, Catholicism is the largest branch of Christianity. Catholicism is by far the majority religion in Latin America (90 percent of the population), in the majority in western Europe (around 60 percent), and a minority religion in North America (25 percent), in black Africa (12 percent), in Asia (4 percent), and in North Africa and the Near and Middle East (2 percent).

The mass, the celebration of the Eucharist

For Catholics, as for other Christians, the risen Christ forms a link between God and people. On Sundays, Catholics celebrate this article of faith together at mass. The mass has two key moments: the reading of the Bible (Old and New Testament) and the sacrament of the eucharist, which Catholics regard as their greatest gift. This is the reenactment of Jesus' last meal with his disciples, during which he established the New Covenant between God and men. It is also for Catholics (and for Orthodox Christians) the mystery of the "real presence" of Christ in the bread and wine. The priest gives the bread to the faithful in the form of a host, a round piece of unleavened bread. Thus, the faithful share, since the beginning of Christianity, in the sacrifice of Christ, who gave his life for humanity.

The place of worship: the church

The church is the place where Catholics meet to pray and worship. It is also a sacred place, where they believe that Christ is

present during the sacrament of the eucharist. The first churches had a floor plan in the shape of a cross. The priest celebrates mass at the altar, a simple table of stone or wood on which are set the Bible, the crucifix, and candles. Beside the altar, a candle is lit on Easter Sunday and on each celebration throughout the year. Behind the altar is the tabernacle, a small coffer in which the hosts are sometimes kept. Churches are decorated with pictures, stained-glass windows, and sculptures that depict the life of Christ, the Virgin Mary, and the saints.

the congregation leaving a church on Sunday

ordination of priests

Ritual and teaching

The Catholic Church recognizes the same sacraments as the Orthodox Church. It does not, however, permit divorce, while Orthodox Christians are permitted to divorce once during their lives. The major festivals are the same. As in the Orthodox Church, the most important festival is Easter, the festival of the resurrection of Christ, although particular emphasis is placed on Christmas, on December 25. The Virgin Mary is greatly venerated. On August 15, Catholics celebrate the Assumption, the ascent of the Virgin to heaven. They also celebrate the saints on All Saints Day, November 1. On November 2, the faithful pray for the dead who are awaiting resurrection. At birth, a child is baptized and thus becomes part of the Christian community. The priest pours water over the child's head as a symbol of purification and anoints it with holy oil. Children receive a religious education called "catechism": they learn to pray to God and to behave in a Christian manner. They take their "first communion," then their "profession of faith" (renewal of the baptism vows), and receive the sacrament of confirmation (the gift of the Holy Spirit).

The hierarchical structure of the Church

In the Catholic Church, the responsibility for interpreting and teaching the Word of God as revealed in the Bible is entrusted to all the bishops, under the authority of the pope. The Vatican II council (1965) reaffirmed that the pope is the "vicar of Christ" and the "shepherd of the whole Church." He has supreme and universal authority in which the bishops join. The pope may call councils, assemblies of all the bishops, which have the power to issue and amend the Church's regulations. He can also convene synods, which are more frequent, but which can only issue proposals. The bishop is "the overseer," the head of a diocese, a regional community. He ordains priests, each of whom is responsible for a parish where he preaches, teaches, and administers the sacraments. Catholic priests are celibate, apart from those in some Oriental churches. They are assisted by deacons, who may be married. The Vatican II council placed more importance on the laity (from the Greek, "people"), encouraging ordinary Catholics to participate in certain religious tasks. This has been mainly applied in the churches of Latin America. The religious orders and religious congregations have an important duty to pray, teach, and help the disadvantaged. Priests, monks, and nuns, and laity constitute the Church. □

Pope John Paul II

Karol Wojtyla, born in Poland in 1920, has been pope since 1978. As bishop of Rome, the pope is regarded as the successor of Peter, Jesus' first apostle. He is elected by important leaders of the Church, the cardinals, by a secret vote.

A priest performs a baptism.

51

Jerusalem

For Jews, Christians, and Muslims, Jerusalem is a holy city. In the foreground is the Western Wall (also known as the Wailing Wall) where Jews assemble to pray. The wall is all that remains of the Temple built by King Herod. Its site is on the rock on which, according to the Bible, Abraham carried out his sacrifice (see inset above). According to Muslim tradition, the prophet Mohammed was conveyed here by the angel Gabriel. A mosque, the Mosque of the Rock, was built on the spot. Its gilded dome can be seen in the picture. Jerusalem is also a holy city for Christians, for it was there that Jesus was crucified, entombed, and resurrected.

Islam, the religion of the Muslims, is based on the belief in one God, Allah, who made himself known to the prophet Mohammed in the 7th century. His revelation to Mohammed was transcribed in a book, the Koran.

Islam

- **ablution:** ritual washing by followers of some religions to purify themselves, by sprinkling water over various parts of their body.
- **jihad:** a holy war that every Muslim must wage to defend or, possibly, extend the domain of Islam. For many Muslims, war is a lesser jihad, the greater jihad being the struggle against evil, including the evil hidden in the heart of the believer.
- **pilgrimage:** a journey believers make to a holy place for religious reasons.
- **prophet:** someone who has been called by God, who listens to the call, and who transmits it to others by words, deeds, and, at times, silences.
- **Ramadan:** the name of the ninth month of the Muslim calendar, during which Mohammed was first visited by the angel Gabriel. It is a period of fasting that enables the believer to become closer to the poor by experiencing like them hunger and thirst.
- **Shiite:** a Muslim who belongs to Shiism, a minority group within Islam.
- **shrine:** building consecrated to religious ceremonies: holy place.
- **Sunnite:** a Muslim who belongs to the Sunni, the majority group within Islam.

In the 6th century A.D., the people living in the Arabian peninsula (present-day Saudi Arabia) were nomadic herdsmen. Most were polytheists, believing in several gods, but among them were some who already recognized a supreme divinity. In the same region were small communities of Christians and Jews who believed in the one God of the Bible. Some Arab tribes traveled several times a year to Mecca, a great commercial city and renowned religious center. There a **cult** was rendered to the Black Stone, built into the corner of a cube-shaped building, the sanctuary of Kaaba.

Mohammed the prophet

Mohammed (also spelled Mahomet or Muhammad in English) was born about A.D. 570 in Mecca, Arabia. An orphan, he was brought up by his uncle Abu Talib. When he was 25 he married Khadijah, a rich merchant woman. All the sons born from their marriage died young, but they also had four daughters, one of whom was Fatima. Mohammed worked for Khadijah and was considered an honest and respectable member of the community. Like some Christians, Mohammed went on retreats into the desert. One day, when he was 40, he heard a voice and had a vision of the angel Gabriel (*Jibril* in Arabic) who revealed to him the words of God. The messages dictated to him day after day form the Koran. From that moment, Mohammed was the **Prophet** of the one God, Allah. His immediate circle of friends and relatives soon shared his belief, but he aroused opposition from the citizens of Mecca. In 619, his wife died. He then took two wives, the younger of whom was Aisha, aged 9, the daughter of one of his first followers, Abu Bakr.

the library inside a mosque

The Hegira

Because of hostility from his fellow citizens, Mohammed left Mecca to settle in Medina on September 24, 622. This "migration" is known as the Hegira (*hijrah* in Arabic) and marks the real beginning of the new religion and the starting point of the Muslim calendar. In Medina, Mohammed organized the first community of believers, or Muslims (from Arabic, meaning "one who submits to God"). He converted the whole population while continuing to receive the divine message. He decided that believers should turn toward the sanctuary of Kaaba in Mecca to pray. According to his revelations, the sanctuary had been built by Abraham and his son Ishmael on the instructions of Allah. Several battles took place between the Muslims and the opponents of the Prophet, notably the inhabitants of Mecca, who submitted, however, in 630. Mohammed died in 632, after making a **pilgrimage** to Mecca.

The two main branches of Islam

After the Prophet's death, disagreements broke out regarding who should succeed him. In 632, the majority of believers thought that the most worthy Muslim should be appointed as the Prophet's successor, whether or not he was a relative of Mohammed. The choice then fell on Abu Bakr, who became the first caliph, the religious and political head of the community. Two other caliphs succeeded him, Omar and Othman. The fourth caliph was Ali, who was the Prophet's son-in-law through his marriage to Fatima. Some Muslims contested his authority, however, because it was more important for them for the leader to be a good Muslim than a relative of the Prophet. This provoked a civil war, which led to the assassination of Ali in 661. This is how the two great branches of the Islamic world emerged: the **Sunnites**, who represent "the people of the community and the tradition" (in Arabic, *sunna*), and the **Shiites**, for whom the descendants of Ali are more appropriate to guide the community. Shiites today make up 12 percent of Muslims, the great majority of whom are Sunnites.

Modern Islam

Islam now has more than 1 billion followers, spread over the entire world. The countries around Arabia (including Egypt, North Africa, Syria, and Iraq) remain the historic and religious heart of Islam. However, Arabs represent only 20 percent of all Muslims. Most Muslims live in Asia (including Indonesia, India, Pakistan, and Bangladesh). Islam also has a great number of followers in black Africa. Arabic, the language in which the Koran was revealed to Mohammed, remains the sacred language of Islam, in which all Muslims must recite their prayers. ☐

the sanctuary of Kaaba

The Expansion of Islam

After the death of Mohammed in 632, the Muslims embarked on conquests to spread the new religion, beginning a formidable expansion. Through war and conversion, Islam spread from Arabia toward distant countries: North Africa, Syria, Persia, Egypt, Spain, and Portugal. At the end of the 8th century, Muslims held sway over an immense empire that stretched from the Atlantic to the frontiers of China. This empire rapidly broke up into a number of states of which the principal capitals were Baghdad, Damascus, and Cordoba. From the 10th to the 15th centuries, Islam spread to the north of India, China, and Central Asia. The capitals of this new Muslim world were Samarkand, Istanbul, and Delhi.

prayer at sunset

The foundations of the Muslim religion

The Shiites

The Shiites (Arabic for "partisans") claim allegiance to Ali, Mohammed's son-in-law. As followers of Ali and his son Hussein, they believe that the best guides of the Islamic community are the imams (religious leaders) who are the successors of Ali and Hussein,

and thus of the Prophet. Above, a miniature picture shows the death of Ali and Hussein, as imagined by an artist. Over time, the Shiites have split into different sects distributed over several countries of the Middle East. They form the majority in Iran and are numerous in Iraq, Pakistan, and Lebanon. Najaf and Karbala, the towns in Iraq where Ali and Hussein were murdered, are holy places for Shiites. In Iran, the Shiite clergy form an independent group that includes the mullahs and the ayatollahs. Ayatollahs interpret religious law and govern society.

The word *Islam* is Arabic for "voluntary submission to a single universal God" and characterizes the attitude that the Muslim believer must have toward Allah, the one God. Islam is a religion based on the texts of the Koran and the Sunna. These contain a body of rules, known as Islamic law or "Sharia," which regulate everyday life.

The Koran and the Sunna

In Arabic, *koran* means "reading," "book," or "recitation." When the angel Gabriel revealed the words of God to Mohammed, he ordered him to repeat them, saying, "Recite." Mohammed learned these texts by heart and dictated them to his companions, who transcribed them on palm leaves, pieces of leather, and camels' shoulder blades. After the Prophet's death, the caliph Othman finished compiling the texts that were to constitute the Koran. The Koran comprises 6,226 verses, divided into 114 suras or chapters. It is written in Arabic, the language in which the revelation was received. The sacred book of Islam is complemented by another body of texts called the *Sunna* Sitas (Arabic for "custom" or "tradition"). The Sunna is made up of the words, actions, and opinions of Mohammed: the *hadiths* or "words of the Prophet," which were collected by his companions. The Koran and the Sunna constitute the basis of the faith and law, guiding the life of each believer.

The message of the Koran

The Koran repeats with insistence that there is only one God, Allah. The creator and savior of the Universe, he is inaccessible and cannot be represented in images. The Koran states that this God has transmitted his word and law to various prophets, including Abraham, Moses, Jesus, and Mohammed.

a page of the Koran

However, no other divine revelation can override that which Mohammed received, because this revelation encompasses and surpasses all that have gone before.

The five pillars of Islam

The five fundamental duties of each Muslim, known as the five pillars of Islam, are the following:
– The profession of faith of the believer, called the *shahada*, is expressed in these words: "There is no god but Allah and Mohammed is his servant and his prophet." It is proclaimed five times a day from the top of the minaret when the muezzin calls the faithful to prayer.

a pool for ablutions, inside a mosque

– Ritual prayer must be performed by each believer five times a day, at dawn, at midday, in the middle of the afternoon, at sunset, and when night has fallen.

– Legal alms, known as *zakat*, are a religious tax that a Muslim must set aside from his salary or harvest to help the poor.

– During the month of **Ramadan**, adults must abstain from drinking, eating, smoking, and sexual intercourse from dawn to sunset. In the evening each family breaks the fast and meets to pray and eat dinner.

– The great pilgrimage to Mecca is a journey that every Muslim must make at least once during his lifetime, if he has the health and means to do so, to demonstrate his faith. **Jihad** literally means "the fight for a just cause," but it is usually translated incorrectly as "holy war." It is not one of the pillars of

studying the Koran in a Koranic school

Islam, but it is often considered to be a religious obligation.

The Islamic law or Sharia

The Islamic law or Sharia is contained in the Koran and the Sunna. It governs social and family life and lays down all rituals from birth to death. The rules of the Sharia are not applied in the same way in all Muslim countries. In some states, the Sharia is applied literally and is the only source of laws and regulations. These can sometimes be very severe, and guilty persons may be sentenced to corporal punishments. In other Muslim states, specialists in Islam research ways of adapting Muslims to the realities of modern life, while remaining faithful to the teachings of the Koran. Whatever their attitude toward Muslim traditions, all followers of Islam mark the stages of life in the same way. Muslim boys must be circumcised, following a tradition that predates Islam. The religious education of children begins with the reading of the Koran at Koranic schools. Marriage is a family ceremony. At burial, the deceased is placed with the head turned toward Mecca. The Sharia also contains rules concerning food. A Muslim must not eat the meat of an animal slaughtered without the recitation of a ritual formula, nor must he or she consume pork or alcohol. □

Muslim women

Having arisen at the beginning of the Middle Ages, Islamic law has kept characteristics of that period. It limits the freedom of women who, according to this law, must behave in such a way as to not commit any transgressions against men. Since in the Middle Ages it was not proper for them to go bareheaded, women in some Muslim countries—not in all—wear a veil (called the chador in Iran and the hijab in North Africa), like these students at the University of Cairo. The Koran provides women with

protection that they did not have in earlier times. It affirms that "he who brings up two girls will go to Paradise." It obliges men to treat their wives correctly. It authorizes polygamy but limits it to four wives, with the condition that each wife approves and that each is afforded the same standing.

pilgrims circling the Kaaba, in Mecca, Saudi Arabia

Practices and festivals

Muslim ceremonies usually take place in the mosque. There are solemn prayers on Friday (a day of prayer, but not a day of obligatory rest) and the religious festivals that mark the Muslim calendar. In addition, the faithful must pray five times daily, no matter where they may be.

Religious leaders

Islam accepts no intermediary between man and God. The religious service is conducted by a respected member of the community who is learned in the Muslim faith. Often the person responsible for presiding over collective prayer is an imam, an Arabic word that means "leader." Under his direction, at midday on Fridays, the faithful meet to pray and listen to a sermon. In Shiite Islam, the term *imam* has a special meaning. It describes the descendants of the Prophet who were supreme leaders of the whole community of believers, the first of whom, after Mohammed, was Ali. Specialists in the Koran and Islamic law, for example, ulemas and muftis, are entrusted with special roles in Islam. In the Muslim world, there is no central authority that pronounces on questions of faith.

The mosque

The mosque is the building where Muslims meet, mainly to pray. It is often decorated with verses of the Koran painted or carved in stone but has no figurative representation. In the Muslim religion, God cannot be shown. Only his words are illustrated. The entrance to a mosque is generally through a wide courtyard that contains the pool for **ablutions**. Each believer must sprinkle water over his hands, arms, face, head, and feet to purify himself before going to pray.

The Muslim festivals

Ritual practices, festivals, and even Islamic civil life are regulated by a calendar that differs from that of Christian countries. Its starting point is the year 622 of the Christian era, the date of the Hegira, Mohammed's flight to Medina. Muslim festivals occur throughout the calendar's twelve months, which alternate between 29 and 30 days. During the month of Ramadan, the Night of Destiny, *Lailat-al-Qadr*, is celebrated, recalling the revelation of the Koran to Mohammed. The festival of *Id al-Fitr*, or Small Festival, brings the Ramadan fast to an end. It is a joyful festival on which, in every house, cakes are shared and presents given out. At the end of the pilgrimage to Mecca the "Feast of the Sheep" takes place (see next paragraph).

Pilgrimage to Mecca

The last month of the Muslim year is *Dhu al-Hijja*, or the month of pilgrimage, dedicated to pilgrimage to Mecca. Mecca is the principal holy city of Islam. The others are Medina and Jerusalem (called Al Quds, "the holy one," by Muslims). In the center of Mecca is the Kaaba, the small cubical building that is the most holy place of Islam. According to some, the Black Stone that it contains was brought from Paradise by Adam and sealed in the sanctuary by Abraham and his son Ishmael. Today the Kaaba, veiled in black cloths, is the focus of pilgrimage, one of the five compulsory duties of each Muslim. Before beginning the pilgrimage, the believer must put on two pieces of seamless white cloth. The principal ritual

Minaret and muezzin

One or more towers dominate a mosque. They are minarets, from the top of which the muezzin calls the faithful to prayer five times a day. Every Muslim, whether in the mosque or elsewhere, is thus asked to pray.

The Friday prayers

Muslims go to mosques on Friday at midday to pray together. Below, prayers at the mosque of Essaounna in Rabat, Morocco.

the Ibn Tulun Mosque in Cairo, Egypt

consists in circling the Kaaba seven times, walking to the right of the Black Stone. Each time they pass in front of the sacred stone, the faithful kiss it, touch it, or salute it. This pilgrimage is an opportunity for Muslims from every country to meet and pray together. It ends with the Great Feast, *Id al-Adha* (in North Africa, *Aid-el-Kebir*), also known as the Feast of Sacrifices or Feast of the Sheep. While the pilgrimage is happening in Mecca, Muslims celebrate this event in other regions of the world. Each family sacrifices an animal, usually a sheep, in memory of the animal Abraham burned in place of his son Isaac. The meat must be shared between the family, the neighbors, and the poor. ☐

Prayer before the mihrab

A mihrab is a small niche, often richly decorated, hollowed out of the wall at the back of the mosque. It indicates the direction of Mecca, the holiest city of the Muslims. During the service, the faithful line up in rows behind each other and pray facing the mihrab. Before beginning to pray, the believer must purify himself with water and take off his shoes. This is a sign of respect toward God. During prayer, the believer stands up, bows, and then prostrates himself to show his submission to the will of God. Lastly, the person praying sits and recites phrases that express the fundamental truths of Islam.

When praying, Muslims always turn to face Mecca.

n religions

Hinduism is one of the world's oldest religions. It emerged around 2000 B.C. in India, where it is still the majority religion. It is based on sacred texts, and its followers are called Hindus.

Hinduism

- **ablution:** ritual washing by followers of some religions to purify themselves by sprinkling water over various parts of their body.
- **attribute:** trait that is inherent in, or that characterizes, someone or something.
- **avatar:** name given to the various incarnations of the god Vishnu.
- **Brahman:** a member of the highest caste of the Hindus. Brahmans study the sacred texts.
- **caste:** a group into which a person is born and that cannot be changed later in life.
- **epic:** a long poem or prose recitation that recounts the exploits of a legendary hero.
- **guru:** in India, a wise man regarded as a spiritual teacher; he is entrusted with the education of young boys belonging to the higher castes.
- **incarnation:** for a god, taking on the body of a man or an animal.
- **karma:** the principle according to which a human life is only a link in a chain of lives. Happiness in each life depends on the actions in the previous life.
- **reincarnation:** coming back to life after death in a different body.

the supreme god, Brahma

the god Krishna and his companion Rada

Today the Hindu religion has some 750 million followers worldwide. It is dominant in southeast Asia, especially in India and Bali. Hinduism is based on several categories of texts. Chief among them are the Vedas first composed around 1800 B.C. and the **epics**, written from 700 B.C. on.

The sacred texts and the epics

The Vedas recount the origins of the world and the lives of the gods and teach the prayers and rituals. They are made up of four books. The oldest is the Rig Veda, which contains more than a thousand chants addressed to the gods. Comments on the Vedas by **Brahmans** gave rise to other texts, including the Upanishads, the Brahmana, and the Code (or law book) of Manu in which the principle of **castes** and the law of **reincarnation** are explained. The epics were written, usually in verse, after the Vedas. They recount the life of the gods and the origins of the world. The two principal stories are the Mahabharata and the Ramayana. The Mahabharata is the longest poem ever composed. In 200,000 verses, it tells of the struggle between two princely families, the hundred Kauravas and their cousins, the five Pandava brothers. The gods take part in these struggles, including Krishna, who supports the five brothers and helps them to win. In the course of this epic, Krishna imparts his teachings in a long poem, the Bhagavad Gita, or Song of the Blessed One. The Ramayana tells of the life and adventures of Rama, the seventh **incarnation** or **avatar** of the god Vishnu.

the god Vishnu at rest

A multitude of gods

There are several thousand gods in Hinduism. All are representations of a single being that existed before everything and that is found everywhere. At the time when the Vedas were written, Indra, the lord of the sky, was one of the principal gods. Three gods later took on greater importance, Brahma, Vishnu, and Shiva. Brahma creates the world. He has four faces and four arms that enable him to see and to act everywhere. Vishnu preserves the world; his emblems are a disc, symbol of divine energy; a club, symbol of power; and a shell, which represents water, fertility, and riches. Shiva destroys the world to transform it. He is terrifying and benevolent at the same time. He is often represented in a circle of fire, a destructive element, and holds a small drum that produces the first sound, the sound of creation.

The castes

In India, society is divided into castes. At the top are the Brahmans, then the Kshatriya (nobles and warriors), the Vaisya (merchants and farmers), and finally the Sudra (servants of other castes). It was the god Brahma, creator of the world, who instituted this social organization, each caste being derived from a part of his body. From his mouth came the purest caste, that of the Brahmans who study the sacred texts; from his arms the Kshatriya were born; from his thigh, the Vaisya; and from his feet, the Sudra. Hindus who do not belong to any of the four principal castes are regarded as impure and called untouchables. The caste system was officially abolished in 1947 but still exists in some areas.

The cycle of reincarnations

In Hinduism, each individual has several lives. Death is the transit from one destiny to another. After death, the soul, which is eternal, is reincarnated in another body, which will vary depending on the actions accomplished in the life just completed. This is the law of **karma**. □

a holy man at prayer

The god Ganesha

According to legend, Ganesha was keeping watch while his mother, the goddess Parvati, was bathing. His father, the god Shiva, did not recognize him, and in jealousy, cut off his head. To console his wife,

Shiva promised to give Ganesha the head of the first animal that appeared. This was an elephant. Ganesha is thus represented with the body of a pot-bellied man, the head of an elephant, and four arms, and he is usually colored red. He rides on a rat, the symbol of thieves. He is the Lord of Obstacles, the god of knowledge, intelligence, arts, and commerce. This secondary god is one of the most popular Hindu gods, and his birthday is celebrated with major festivals.

Hindus at prayer in a temple

Ritual and festivals

For Hindus, every action in life has a sacred character. Each person is free to approach whichever god they chose from among all the deities of Hinduism, and each day in their homes they make prayers and offerings and perform ablutions. They visit the temple where the priests maintain the cult of their god. They join in festivals and in pilgrimages, through which they may approach nearer to the gods and earn a better reincarnation in a future existence.

Prayers and ceremonies

Each house has an altar with images of the deity that protects the family. Family members pray before the altar twice a day, at dawn and at dusk. Sitting cross-legged, each person recites sacred texts while burning incense sticks and then offers the god

food, flowers, water, seeds, and so forth. Numerous rites of purification punctuate the day, such as rinsing the mouth and sprinkling water over the head. They are accompanied by prayers. Hindus go to the temple in their district or village to visit the gods, to bring them offerings of lamps or lighted candles, fruit, flower or perfumes, and to listen to recitation of the Vedas. A temple is the residence of a principal god, such as Vishnu or Shiva, usually surrounded by other gods associated with them. The image, generally a statue, is kept in a special room and watched over by a temple priest. In large temples, the priest belongs to the caste of the Brahmans. Each day, he "wakes" the god and presents offerings so that the god may look kindly on the whole community of believers. He sings hymns and organizes spectacles of music and dance in the god's honor.

The Ganges

The Ganges is the sacred river. Hindus believe that Ganga Mai, "our mother Ganges," was sent to earth by Brahma. They also believe that its source springs from the big toe of the god Vishnu or that it flows from the hair of Shiva. Its course is dotted with holy cities, particularly Benares or Varanasi. Millions of pilgrims travel to the river for ritual bathing.

Bathing in the River Ganges is a way to purify oneself.

an offering of candles and flowers

In India the cow is a sacred animal, venerated as a symbol of the universe.

The key stages in the life of a believer

After birth, a newborn baby is presented to the gods. On this occasion, a **guru**, or spiritual teacher, goes to the family home and feeds the child with a paste of honey and melted butter. On the tenth day the child is named. When a child is four the head is shaved and the hair offered to the family gods. The hair that grows back will be the sign of a new life. In families belonging to one of the three leading castes, young boys between the ages of seven and ten undergo the initiation ceremony, the *upanayana*, which makes them a full member of their caste. The guru chosen by the father passes the sacred string around the right arm and head of the young Hindu, showing that he is "twice born." Marriage rites last for several days.

The bride is led to her new dwelling carrying new fire for the home, then sits on a red ox skin and shares dishes made as offerings with her husband. A married man, who becomes head of the family, has the duty to produce sons to ensure the family line to look after the family home and to carry out domestic rituals.

Hindu festivals

Festivals take different forms in different regions of India and generally commemorate episodes from the Mahabharata and Ramayana. In November-December, Diwali, the festival of lights, marks the New Year in the north of India. Thousands of small lamps burn in the windows of houses, around the temples and at the foot of statues of the gods. Fireworks are set off in honor of Vishnu. Holi, in February-March, celebrates the arrival of spring. This joyous festival is dedicated to Kama, the god of love. Bonfires are lit in the streets, and as they pass in procession, people sprinkle red powder and colored water as a sign of renewal. Around India and everywhere that Hindus live, other festivals are held in honor of Kali, the ten-armed goddess, the elephant-headed Ganesha, or Rama, the hero of the Ramayana. During the processions to and from the temples, giant images of the gods are paraded on floats. Most festivals end with bathing for purification, to clean the gods of any impurities that their followers may have transmitted. □

A cremation

A dead person is dressed in new clothes and taken in procession to be cremated. The body is placed on a funeral pyre and burned.

The temple of Kandarya

Built in 1002, this is one of the most beautiful buildings at the Khajuraho site in Madhya Pradesh, India, which has thirty temples.

Jainism and Sikhism are religions practiced in India by fewer than 3 percent of the population. Each is based on the teachings of a wise leader who led an exemplary life and preached his faith.

Jainism and Sikhism

◐ alms: a gift made to the poor.

◐ ascetic: a person who chooses a very austere life and renounces bodily pleasures for moral or religious reasons.

◐ caste: a group into which a person is born and that cannot be changed later in life.

◐ chastity: abstaining from sexual relations.

◐ cremation: the custom of burning the dead.

◐ enlightenment: condition of reaching total understanding of the human soul and of the world.

◐ guru: in India, a wise man regarded as a spiritual teacher: he is entrusted with the education of young boys belonging to the higher castes. Among the Sikhs, gurus are the principal religious authority.

◐ jina: a person who has freed himself from the cycle of reincarnations.

◐ karma: the principle according to which a human life is only a link in a chain of lives. Happiness in each life depends on the actions accomplished in the previous life.

◐ reincarnation: coming back to life after death in a different body.

◐ vegetarian: a person who never eats meat.

Jainism and Sikhism arose in reaction to Hinduism and its **caste** system. Jainism was founded in the 5th century B.C. by Mahavira, known as Jina, the conqueror. Sikhism emerged much later, at the end of the 15th century, under the influence of Guru Nanak.

The birth of Jainism

Around 540 B.C., at the age of 28, Mahavira left his family and for 12 years lived as an **ascetic**, traveling the roads, living off alms, and meditating. At the age of 40, he achieved **enlightenment**. From then until his death, Mahavira dedicated his life to teaching. He taught that each person is responsible for his or her own salvation and can put an end to the cycle of successive rebirths. Mahavira's disciples, in turn, went on to preach Jainism. The texts on

which the religion is based were written down much later, in the 5th century.

The message of Jainism

The fundamental principle of Jainism is non-violence (*ahimsa*), which is demonstrated by respect for all life—human, animal, or vegetable. Some monks wear a veil in front of their mouth, and others sweep the ground before them as they walk or before they sit down to avoid killing even the smallest creature. All Jains are **vegetarians**. They may not work in a number of activities, for example, farming, where in tilling the soil they might injure animals. Monks and nuns live in communities directed by a master. They make a vow of **chastity** and poverty. They must not lie or steal. Believers go to the temples to pray and bring offerings of food, perfume, flowers, or money to the **jina** (persons who have attained perfection). They sit at the foot of the statues, reciting hymns and reading the scriptures. Every twelve years, Jains gather at the foot of the statue of

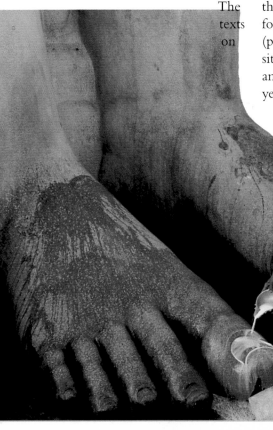

offerings at the feet of the giant statue of Bahubali at Sravanabelgola, a center of pilgrimage in the south of India

a Jain in a temple

Bahubali, a sage who completed the cycle of reincarnations.

The history of Sikhism

When Sikhism emerged, at the end of the 15th century, India had been governed for two centuries by Turkish rulers who sought to impose the Islamic faith. Sikhism takes from Islam its belief in a single god, Mahavira an all-powerful creator. The founder of Sikhism was Guru Nanak, who was born near Lahore in the Punjab in 1469. After several years of meditation and wandering, one day he gained enlightenment. He then began to preach his faith in a supreme god and taught how to escape from the law of **karma** by freeing oneself from the cycle of **reincarnations**. His disciples were called Sikhs, meaning "those who have learned." By his death in 1539, he had become the **guru**, or spiritual leader, of a new religion. Nine gurus followed him in succession, enriching Sikhism with their teachings. All of these texts, amounting to more than 1,400 pages, constitute the Granth Sahib, the Sikh's sacred book. In the 18th century, the tenth guru, Govind Singh, transformed Sikhism into a religion of warriors with a code of discipline. The religion was known as "the religion of kirpan," meaning the sword, opposed Muslim domination, and affirmed that everyone is equal irrespective of their caste of origin. Govind Singh declared that after him religious authority would no longer derive from a guru but from the book itself. Thus the Granth Sahib became the Guru Granth Sahib.

Sikh rites and festivals

A Sikh's life is marked by four principal rites: the choosing of a name, initiation during adolescence, marriage, and **cremation** after death. Certain clothes and accessories are part of ritual. The five Ks, uncut beard and hair (*kesh*), fastened by a comb (*kangha*), metal bracelet (*kara*), short trousers (*karsha*), and the sword (*kirpan*), represent both the unity and fraternity of the Sikh community. They also remind believers that they must defend their rights and liberty. The sacred book is at the heart of Sikh ritual. Each home has a copy. In Sikh temples, the Guru Granth Sahib rests on an altar covered by a cloth to protect it from impurities. Sikhs go to the temples to listen to sacred prayers and hymns. ☐

Zoroastrianism

Zoroastrianism is a religion founded in Persia (modern Iran) in the 5th century B.C. by Zoroaster. In the 9th century, many Zoroastrians settled in the northwest of India where they are called Parsis or Parsees (Persians). Their principal god is Ahura-Mazda, whose symbol is fire. Today there are roughly 200,000 Parsis in India.

reading from the Guru Granth Sahib

Buddhism was founded in India in the 5th century B.C. by Buddha, a sage, and spread across Asia between the 2nd and 12th centuries A.D. Buddhism was influenced by the beliefs of the countries that adopted it.

Buddhism

- ◑ **ascetic:** a person who chooses a very austere life and renounces bodily pleasures for moral or religious reasons.
- ◑ **bodhisattva:** a sage who takes a vow to save all beings and to help those who suffer instead of achieving nirvana.
- ◑ **cult:** worship rendered to a god or a deity; ceremony in which that worship is rendered.
- ◑ **doctrine:** a body of beliefs, ideas, and rules, which define a conception of the world and a way of conducting oneself.
- ◑ **enlightenment:** condition of reaching total understanding of the human soul and of the world.
- ◑ **nirvana:** a state achieved when a person, having escaped the cycle of reincarnations, feels no more desire, and therefore no more suffering.
- ◑ **prayer wheel:** a cylinder containing sacred prayers, which Buddhists turn with one hand.
- ◑ **reincarnation:** coming back to life after death in a different body.
- ◑ **ritual:** the totality of religious practices and ceremonies carried out within the framework of a belief or religion.
- ◑ **sermon:** a religious speech.

Buddhism is one of the world's three dominant religions today, with between 300 and 400 million followers, most of whom live in southeast Asia. The founder of Buddhism, the Buddha, was born in India at the end of the 6th century B.C. At that time, all Indians practiced Hinduism, and it was by drawing on that religion that the Buddha taught a new **doctrine**. This was more of a philosophy, without a god or sacred text, than a religion.

The life of the Buddha

Prince Siddharta Gautama was born about 533 B.C. in the town of Kapilavastu, in the north of India. He led a very sheltered existence in the palace of his parents. At the age of 29, however, he had four encounters that changed his life: he came across an old man, a sick man, a corpse, and a monk begging for food. He thus discovered old age, pain, death, and poverty and began to wonder about the meaning of existence. He decided to go out into the world as a wandering monk and to meditate. First, he spent time with Hindu ascetics, who taught him to fast and to concentrate in order to meditate. He then studied the sacred texts of Hinduism. Finding no answer to his questions, he decided to seek within himself for the way to the truth and his own liberation. Legend says that at Bodhgaya he sat at the foot of a fig tree, a tree that symbolizes knowledge (*bodhi*), and after lengthy meditation there gained **enlightenment**. He then became the Buddha, "the awakened one" or "enlightened one." He gave his first sermon at Benares. With his disciples, he then traveled the north of India to teach his doctrine. After long years of wandering, he died at a great age.

The message of the Buddha

During the **sermon** at Benares, the Buddha set out for his followers the Four Noble Truths, which constitute the basis of his teaching. He first affirmed that the world consists only of pain (First Truth). Birth, sickness, old age, and death bring suffering. Pain stems from attachment to life and the desire, which can never be satisfied, to possess

statue of the reclining Buddha, at Polonnaruwa, Sri Lanka

the birth of the Buddha

the Buddha under the fig tree at Bodhgaya, where he achieved enlightenment

The footprints of the Buddha

When Buddhism began, no pictures or statues of Buddha were made because it seemed impossible to depict such an extraordinary figure. Therefore, symbols, such as the tracks he left when passing, were used. In the temple of Haein in Korea, the monks preserve more than 81,000 pieces of wood like the one below.

They represent the footprints of the Buddha and are engraved with sacred texts. Other symbols of the Buddha are the wheel, symbol of life and the cosmos; the parasol and the throne, symbols of authority; the lotus, a flower that symbolizes purity; and the white elephant that Buddha's mother dreamed about before he was born.

happiness (Second Truth). To eliminate pain and achieve peace, it is necessary to free oneself from desire and obliterate it (Third Truth) by leading an exemplary life (Fourth Truth). With the last truth, the Buddha expounded the way that human beings must take to eliminate pain and attain **nirvana**. He defined nirvana as a state of eternal bliss, in which desire, ignorance, time, and suffering no longer exist. With nirvana, the cycle of successive **reincarnations** ended. Buddhism is addressed to everyone without exclusion: whatever their sex or social origin, all Buddhists belong to the same community, the sangha. To achieve wisdom, it is necessary to mediate at length each day on the Four Truths and to follow the moral principles defined by Buddha. In the 3rd century B.C., the Indian emperor Asoka converted to Buddhism, which became the official religion in India. Many monks spread the Buddhist message outside India, and the teaching took hold all over Asia, reaching Sri Lanka, Burma, and China. Until the 8th century, Buddhism expanded very rapidly, taking root in Korea, Japan, and Tibet. However, it began to disappear in India from the 5th century A.D. ☐

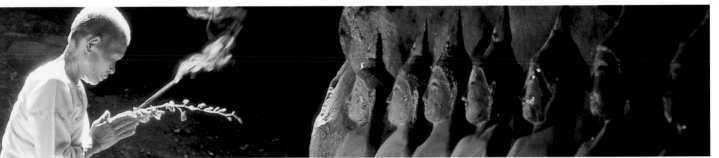

a woman praying before statues of the Buddha

The strands of Buddhism and festivals

Tibetan Buddhism

This form of Buddhism is also known as Lamaism, from the name of the monks, the lamas, who ruled Tibet. Stemming from Mahayana Buddhism, it has blended with older beliefs of the Tibetans. The Dalai Lama is the spiritual head of Tibetan Buddhism and is regarded as a reincarnation of

the Buddha. His palace at Lhasa (top) in Tibet still attracts many believers. The Dalai Lama now lives in exile, because his country has been occupied by China since 1959. Lamaists practice all kinds of rituals to invoke their divinities and to ward off demons. They frequently use prayer wheels, which are sometimes attached to temple entrances, as shown above.

In the 3rd century A.D., Buddhism divided into two major branches, each of which offers a different way or vehicle for achieving nirvana: the Hinayana (the Lesser Vehicle) and the Mahayana (the Great Vehicle). In its beginnings Buddhism had no ceremonies or ritual. However, its followers have gradually developed **ritual** and festivals.

Hinayana Buddhism

The Hinayana branch, or Lesser Vehicle, is today practiced by 35 percent of Buddhists. It is the dominant religion in Sri Lanka, Burma, Thailand, Cambodia, and Laos. Its followers strictly apply the Buddha's rule of life. They commit themselves to finding refuge in the Buddha, in the dharma (Buddha's teachings), and in the sangha (the community). Hinayana Buddhism is in essence a monastic rule of life without a supreme divinity. Believers abide by certain prohibitions: to kill, to steal, to commit

adultery (to be unfaithful), to lie, and to consume alcoholic drinks are all forbidden. Monks choose to retire from society and to live in a community. They have only one meal a day and live from alms—relying on gifts from the public. Monks are responsible for the education of children and officiate at births, marriages, and burials. Every year, there is a festival to celebrate the foundation of the community (in February or March) and the period when the monks stay in the monastery during the rainy season (in July or August).

Mahayana Buddhism

Some 60 percent of modern Buddhists belong to the Mahayana strand (the Great Vehicle), which is mainly practiced in China, Korea, Japan, Nepal, Mongolia, and Vietnam. Mahayana Buddhists interpret the Buddha's message in a wider sense. They also render homage to Hindu gods and to those of other

young Thai monks

a Buddhist makes an offering of incense

religions, such as Taoism in China and Shinto in Japan. They mainly venerate various representations of the Buddha, whom they have made into a god. They also worship the **bodhisattvas**, human beings imbued with wisdom who have decided to consecrate themselves to the salvation of others. The most venerated bodhisattva is Avalokiteshvara, who has many arms and heads, symbolizing the infinite help that he brings to humanity. During ceremonies monks cover the Buddha's statue with cloths, gold, and jewels. The faithful bring offerings of food, flowers, or incense. They recite prayers and seat themselves at the feet of the Buddha to meditate.

The collective festivals

All Buddhists celebrate festivals to commemorate the main events of the Buddha's life. Crowds of believers make pilgrimages to the places where the Buddha lived: Kapilavastu, the town where he was born; Bodhgaya, where he attained enlightenment; Benares, where he preached for the first times; and Kusinara, where he died. In the many temples that have been built at these places, pilgims pray and prostrate themselves before the images of the Buddha. The ritual differs depending on the region or country. The believer may sit cross-legged on the ground with hands on knees, prostrate himself face down on the ground, pray with beads by repeating formulas, or even use a **prayer wheel**. In April, the Buddha's birth is celebrated. In some countries, altars of flowers are set up in temples with statues of the child Buddha over which sugared tea is poured. In July, the Buddha's death is commemorated. On this date Buddhists honor the spirits of the dead by lighting small lamps, which are floated on

a Buddhist funeral procession in Korea

water. The festivals are an occasion for performances. Monks wear masks and costumes to reenact events of Buddha's life and to relive the many legendary tales inspired by it. □

A Stupa

Followers of Mahayana Buddhism venerate relics of the Buddha that were distributed after his death. These relics include such items as bones, hair, and teeth. Monuments or stupas were built to keep them in. Stupas are usually dome-shaped. According to legend, Buddha himself indicated this shape by turning his alms bowl upside down. Stupas also contain the

ashes of bodhisattvas and holy texts. Believers visit them to make offerings. They walk around the building singing hymns and reciting prayers. The eyes of the Buddha are represented on the Great Stupa of Bodnath (above), in Nepal. The symbol between the eyes stands for the Buddha's links with the divine.

The temple of Borobudur

This temple is an important place of pilgrimage. Many Buddhist monks and believers go there to pray and meditate. It is in Java in Indonesia (southeast Asia) and was built in the 8th century. The chief sanctuary is a mandala, which means that it symbolizes the cosmos or universe as the Buddhists represent it. Its four stairways point east, west, north, and south. The first five terraces symbolize the Buddha's life on earth, and the three highest terraces represent the spiritual world. Above is a sculpture of the Buddha carved in the caves of Ajanta, a place of pilgrimage in India.

73

Two religious movements sprang up in China in the 6th century B.C., Confucianism and Taoism. The first was founded by Confucius, the second by Laozi. These two religions or philosophies have endured until today.

Confucianism and

- **cult:** worship rendered to a god or a deity; ceremony in which that worship is rendered.
- **disciple:** a person who follows the instruction of a teacher.
- **doctrine:** a body of beliefs, ideas, and rules, which define a conception of the world and a way of conduct.
- **fast:** abstention from eating for religious reasons.

- **morality:** body of rules of guidance for society, which are based on the concepts of good and evil.
- **ritual:** religious practices and ceremonies carried out within the framework of a belief or religion.
- **tao or dao:** the principle of order that explains the Universe. *Tao* means "the true way that leads to the sky."
- **yang:** see yin.
- **yin:** yin and yang are the two complementary forces, one feminine and one masculine, which prevail in the world. The balance of opposites explains, among other things, the cycle of the seasons.

Other beliefs were prevalent in China even before the advent of Confucianism and Taoism. In the 2nd century B.C., Buddhism arrived from India and was adopted by many Chinese. This religion later became as important as Confucianism and Taoism. For the Chinese, their **doctrines** are not contradictory.

The cult of the ancestors
In ancient China, between the 23rd and 3rd centuries B.C., the predominant religion was the **cult** of the ancestors. The dead were regarded as spirits that kept close links with their living descendants. Each Chinese family venerated its ancestors. In the home, the names of the dead were written on tablets placed on a small altar at which incense sticks were lit and offerings made.

Confucianism
In the 6th century B.C., a sage named Confucius taught a new doctrine. His Chinese name is Kongzi, or Master Kong, and his doctrine is not really a religion but rather a **morality** intended to guide people toward perfection. His teachings were collected in books called the Five Classics and in the Conversations compiled by his **disciples**. Confucius taught respect for **ritual** and filial piety, that is, absolute obedience to the father, who is the supreme authority. Confucianism establishes rules of social life and has no priests, god, or temples. The only cult that it recognizes is the cult of the ancestors. One of its rituals consists in traveling to the tomb of the sovereign to pay homage to him as the ancestor of the community. The ideas of Confucius apply in

Confucian school in a village in Korea

Taoism

a Taoist rite that involves fertilizing
the earth with incense

a meeting of priests during
a Taoist festival

The union of the three doctrines

Buddhism flourished in China alongside Taoism and Confucianism from the 2nd century B.C. The three religions have influenced each other. In the 16th and 17th centuries, a movement even attempted to combine the three doctrines into one. Most Chinese practice all three religions, so it is possible sometimes to see Buddha, Confucius, and Laozi represented side by side (as below). According to legend, Confucius and Laozi met while they were alive. Whether they are Confucians, Taoists, or Buddhists, Chinese travel to the sacred mountain of Tai Shan, on the slopes of which many temples have been built.

a special way to relations between the emperor and his subjects, or between the state and the people. Just as it obliges the son to obey the father, Confucianism recommends obedience to the sovereign. The mandarins, or civil servants, who acted for the emperor in ruling China had to know the texts of Confucius. After the Communist revolution and especially during the regime of Mao Zedong, Confucianism was suppressed. Despite this, many Chinese continue to practice it.

Taoism

Taoism was founded in the 6th century B.C. by a philosopher named Laozi or Lao-tse, which means "old master." Laozi was the author of a small book, the *Tao Te Jing* or *Book of the Way and of Virtue*. In it, he taught Taoism, or the doctrine of the Way (**tao** or dao, in Chinese). Two forces divide and regulate life: **yin**, which is cold, opaque, and feminine, and **yang**, which is hot, luminous, and masculine. These two complementary forces are balanced. Human beings must find their own tao, take their place within the universe, and not destroy the harmony that prevails in it. Taoists venerate the gods of the sky, earth, and water, the forces of the winds, rivers, and mountains. Its followers are mainly peasants and artisans. Each village has a temple of the earth god, protector of the district and its people. In the 2nd century A.D., Taoism became a fully fledged religion with new texts, shrines, and priests. The rules recommend **fasting**, meditation, gentleness, and purity. Believers began to make pilgrimages to holy places such as mountains and islands or wherever a deity dwells to bring offerings and thus win the god's favor. One of the five sacred peaks of Taoism is Tai Shan in the province of Shandong. On the road leading to the summit of the mountain, the faithful burn incense sticks, which they plant along the path. Influenced by Buddhism, some Taoists retire from life and found monasteries. □

The religions of Japan

Shinto and Buddhism are the two main religions of Japan. Shinto began in Japan, while Buddhism arrived there in the 6th century and developed in unique ways.

- ◗ **altar:** table or surface on which offerings to deities are placed or sacrifices are made.
- ◗ **amulet:** an object meant to protect from evil the person who wears it or keeps it near.
- ◗ **bodhisattva:** a sage who takes a vow to save all beings and to help those who suffer instead of achieving nirvana.
- ◗ **cult:** worship rendered to a god or a deity; ceremony in which that worship is rendered.
- ◗ **enlightenment:** condition of reaching total understanding of the human soul and of the world.
- ◗ **kami:** a deity of Shinto. The kami are invisible and cannot be represented. The most important kami is the sun goddess, Amaterasu, whose name means "she who illuminates the sky."
- ◗ **martial arts:** a group of combat sports of Japanese origin, including judo, karate, and aikido.
- ◗ **shrine:** building consecrated to religious ceremonies; holy place.
- ◗ **torii:** a large gate that stands in the sacred area in front of the entrance to Shinto temples.

The oldest religion of Japan is Shinto, which combines the cult of the ancestors with veneration of nature. Its deities are spirits or **kami**. In the 6th century, Buddhism spread into the upper classes of Japanese society. The emperors continued to practice Shintoist rites, however, to avoid offending the people, who mainly remained loyal to the traditional beliefs. In the 19th century, Shinto was proclaimed the national religion. Nowadays, the Japanese mix practices from both religions.

Shintoism

The word "Shinto" means "way of the kami." Originally the kami were the souls of dead ancestors who took shelter in such natural places as waterfalls, ocean waves, or volcano craters. Later, they came to signify those elements possessing extraordinary energy such as the sun, the moon, the trees, or the wind. They can be benevolent or malevolent.

Legends, first written down in the 8th century, recount the creation of the world and the birth of the kami and of Japan. The kami use messengers: the fox is the messenger of Inari, who protects men from evil and brings riches. The kami are consulted at

The fox, messenger of the kami Inari

every opportunity, such as before a journey or an examination, to cure a sick person, to curse an enemy, to ward off bad luck, or to have a child.

The Shinto shrine

In Japanese homes there is a small **altar** dedicated to the family kami and before which **amulets** are placed. These amulets are usually wooden arrows or strips of paper bearing the name of a famous **shrine**. A shrine is the residence of the kami of a place. The believer who goes to invoke a spirit first crosses the great gateway, the **torii**, which marks the entrance to the sacred space. Then he purifies himself by rinsing his mouth and washing his hands in a basin or in a natural spring within the shrine. He then goes into the room for worship (*haiden*) but does not enter the principal room (*honden*) because this is the home of the kami. After dropping a coin in the offering box, he rings the bell and claps his hands three times to advise the kami of his presence. Then he bows and recites his prayer.

Pure Land and Zen Buddhism

Arriving from China and Korea, Buddhism spread to Japan at the end of the 6th century and gave rise to various schools derived from the Mahayana branch (the Great Vehicle). The most popular form of Buddhism in Japan is Pure Land Buddhism, venerating the Buddha Amida. It emerged in India and reached Japan in the 10th century. Buddha Amida is the Buddha of infinite light and is honored by repeating phrases such as "Glory to the Buddha Amida."

Zen Buddhism, which flourished from the 12th century, was also imported from China and has had great influence. Its purpose is to achieve enlightenment through intense

A Shintoist purification beneath a waterfall

meditation and severe physical discipline. Practicing martial arts, contemplating a garden of sand, and meditating for several hours are all methods of Zen. The spirit of Zen manifests itself in the tea ceremony and in the art of flower arranging, known as "ikebana."

Ceremonies, festivals, and pilgrimages

Buddhism and Shinto are closely interwoven. Under the influence of Buddhism, kamis have become the patron gods of temples and are represented with attributes of bodhisattvas. Buddhist monks also participate in Shinto festivals. The Japanese marry in Shinto shrines and celebrate funerals in Buddhist monasteries.

To fulfil a vow or to gain salvation for themselves or for someone who has died, the Japanese go on pilgrimages to holy places or shrines where the deities reside. In shrines or before statues they leave messages on which are written their name and their wishes. To invoke the kami of the mountains or that of the village and to ensure its goodwill, the Japanese organize festivals such as the spring and new year festivals. These generally include performances of dancing or sumo wrestling and archery competitions.

Votive offerings to Inari

These are objects or strips of paper (above) left in a shrine by the faithful to thank a god or to make a request.

Position of the hands in Zen meditation

This traditional position taken during meditation is called "Hakkaiyo-in," which signifies the universe.

It is one of the mudras, symbolic gestures of the hands, with special positions of the fingers. Each of these positions has a religious meaning and expresses a particular sentiment.

Zen monk meditating before a garden of sand

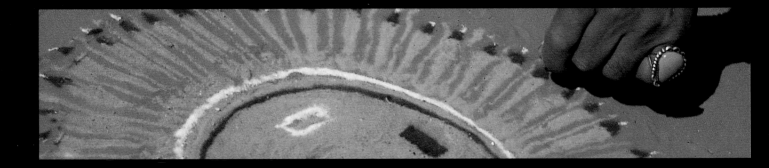

onal beliefs

African beliefs traditionally were handed down by word of mouth. They were recited by the guardians of tradition, storytellers known as griots. These stories were never written down in books.

African religions

- **animism: a belief that attributes souls to animals and to natural phenomena and objects.**
- **circumcision: operation that consists in cutting away the fold of skin covering the glans of the penis.**
- **deity: divine being, either god or goddess.**
- **ethnic: describes a group whose members have the same language, culture, and traditions.**
- **fetish: an object to which magic or supernatural properties are attributed.**
- **griot: in black Africa, a person who knows and recounts the ancient myths and stories.**
- **ritual: religious practices and ceremonies carried out within the framework of a belief or religion.**
- **sacrifice: offering made to a deity, often by killing animals.**
- **sorcerer: an individual who can make contact with the gods and forces of nature. He uses magical practices (such as charms and spells) on human beings, animals, or plants.**
- **trance: state of exaltation of a person transported beyond self and the real world. This state can be achieved by taking substances or by dancing.**

The countries of black Africa are inhabited by many **ethnic** groups. The Bantus (about 60 million) live in central and southern Africa. In the west, among other Sudanese groups live the Bambaras and the Dogons. Besides the major groups, there are smaller isolated groups such as the Pygmies of the

A Bantu dancer in costume; the cauldron on his head symbolizes a volcano.

rain forest and the Bushmen of the deserts of southwest Africa. These various peoples developed different beliefs. Hunting peoples, for instance, needed to stay in the favor of the animal-gods, whom they regarded as their distant relatives, to make hunting possible. Agricultural peoples had all sorts of gods to help them at sowing or harvest time. All traditional African religions are rooted in closeness to nature, the mysteries of which are explained by invisible forces; this is known as **animism**.

A creator god and other deities

In most of the religions of black Africa, believers hold that the world was created by a single, distant god, who pays scant attention to humans. This creator god—called Amma among the Dogon—is rarely depicted. Generally, the creator god gives birth to a god or to a hero, who teaches people all their skills. For example, according to the Bambaras, Faro, the water god, gave life to the earth and then defeated Pemba, the god of the earth, spreading life throughout the world. This civilizing god is at the top of a pyramid of **deities**. Africans often believe that these deities are ancestors or kings who became gods after their death and inhabit the bush and forests, where they live with various spirits.

They are represented by statues and masks. The stories of the gods are told, or at times sung, by wandering storytellers known as **griots**.

Sacrifices to the gods

Religion is present at all times in the lives of Africans, since all nature

ritual dance in the Ivory Coast

has a divine soul. Ceremonies bring believers closer to the deities and to their ancestors, who help them at the important times of life: birth, marriage, death, harvest, or departure for hunting. During these ceremonies, sacrifices for the benefit of gods and people are made. The person making the sacrifice pours millet gruel over the ground or cuts the throat of a small animal, whose blood feeds the god. By eating what remains of the gruel, or the meat of the animal, human beings are revitalized by the god, who keeps bad luck and sickness away from their lives.

Initiation

Initiation is a rite by which an individual is admitted into a group. At puberty, for example, young boys must prove that they are capable of behaving as adults: they must provide for their own needs, alone in the bush or the forest, and prove that they can resist pain by undergoing **circumcision**. The secrets of the group are revealed only to the initiated: these concern not only the gods but also skills and know-how. Thus, after the initiation of adolescent girls, mature women reveal the secrets of sex and childbirth to them. The end of each rite is marked by great festivals, during which statues and masks of the ancestors are used to communicate with their spirits. Initiation ceremonies, which determine a person's place in society, are still important today.

Magic and trances

A traditional part of African belief is that people can compel the forces of nature to do their will. To do so, they must know spells or possess objects that give those using them powers equal to those of the deities. These objects or **fetishes** may be statues representing the dead or statues containing

mysterious substances. Masks of the gods or ancestors can also give magical powers temporarily to their wearers. Africans also believe that men can communicate directly with the gods. To do so, they must cease to be ordinary human beings and be "brought outside of themselves" by an exaltation that they consider supernatural, a **trance**. When a deity enters a person in a trance, that person is "possessed" and behaves in an

a Dogon griot in Mali

extraordinary way. A trance can either take possession of a **sorcerer**, or priest, a person whose role is to communicate with the gods, or of groups, indeed, of a whole village. □

Dance mask

Masks are often used to relive the myths or exploits of the ancestors. For instance, by acting out in masks a victory from the past, some Ivory Coast peoples believe that they can protect their village from present enemies.

A reliquary

This object sits atop a type of basket in which human relics are kept.

The religions of Ocean

❶ ethnic: describes a group whose members have the same language, culture, and traditions.

❶ mana: among the Melanesians, a supernatural, invisible force that is a source of hidden energy. It passes power on to certain objects, to totems, for instance.

❶ myth: legendary tale that seeks to explain the origin of humankind or of the world.

❶ ritual: religious practices and ceremonies carried out within the framework of a belief or religion.

❶ sorcerer: an individual who can make contact with the gods and forces of nature. He uses magical practices (such as charms and spells) on human beings, animals, or plants.

❶ taboo (from the Polynesian tapu "forbidden, sacred"): the characteristic of an object, person, act, or place considered forbidden or dangerous.

❶ tiki: statue or carved object that can represent ancestors.

❶ totem: an animal or plant that a tribe or a clan regards as its ancestor or protector; a representation, usually in the form of a post, of that ancestor.

sacred python painted on eucalyptus bark by Australian Aboriginals

Oceania, the world's fifth "continent," is the least populated continent in the world. Located in the south of the Pacific Ocean, it is made up of the huge island of Australia and several archipelagos, or groups of islands, including Polynesia and Melanesia.

The Aboriginals of Australia

Australia is a huge island, virtually a continent (it is roughly the same size as the United States without Alaska). The Aboriginals, who lived there, before Europeans arrived, still subsist partly from hunting, fishing, and gathering. Despite their varying environments and ways of living, the beliefs of different ethnic groups—which are transmitted orally—have points in common. The Dream Time, Alcheringa, is the beginning of time, the time of creation, when the gods and heroes of myths were born. These heroes, both men and women, fashioned Australia's landscape with their own hands and gave birth to the human species. Then, worn out, they disappeared. Some gods returned to the sky, which man cannot reach, while others still inhabit certain places on earth, which remain sacred. These sacred places are forbidden—they are **taboo**. The most important of them is Ayers Rock, the home of the dead ancestors. Also, each man and each woman is linked to a god or an ancestor by an animal emblem, their **totem**. The Australian Aboriginals believe that during the Dream Time, the gods taught men the rituals that they use today to relive this extraordinary period, and thus to reinforce their vital energy. By living the Dream Time again, human beings come into contact with the creator gods and the ancestors who occupy the taboo places and

a inhabitant of Papua New Guinea decorated for a ceremony

objects. The rituals, which are reserved for certain groups, consist of chants, dances, and the use of sacred objects. Those involving men are taboo for women, and vice versa. Aborigine **sorcerers** employ magical practices to help people through the important stages of life such as birth, puberty, and death.

Polynesia

Polynesia includes Hawaii, Easter Island, New Zealand, and Tahiti, among many other islands. This group of islands has a "native" population of almost 500,000 people whose ancestors came to the islands within the past 10,000 years. The Polynesians all believe in a supreme god—whom they call Tangaroa, Tangaola, or Taaroa—who created the world. Creation myths differ from one region to another: in one place, tradition says that he fished the islands from the sea, in another that he fashioned them from shellfish. He also created other gods, for example, Tane, god of light and canoe building, and Rongo, god of peace, poetry, and agriculture. The ancestor cult is very important. The New Zealand Maoris claim descent from the crew of the Waka, the original canoe that brought the first human beings. The world of the living is always in contact with that of the dead. It is believed that the dead can exercise their power at any time and can be friendly or hostile, depending on whether they are content or not. In festivals, the dead are honored and represented by paintings, masks, and ornaments made of shells. Priests are responsible for seeing that rites are properly carried out and taboos respected. Cult places are quite varied: they include the men's house, reserved for special rites; the house of the ancestors, possibly decorated with their

a female tiki

tikis; the house of canoes; and taboo places in the wild.

Melanesia

Melanesia is the largest island group within Oceania (with four million inhabitants). It includes the Fiji Islands, Vanuatu, New Caledonia, and Papua New Guinea. In Melanesia, the creator gods, who show little concern about what they have created, are unimportant. Cults center on the heroes who taught people arts and skills. These are often two brothers who did not agree and founded rival clans, or twin and opposed gods who are hot and cold, male and female, dry and wet. Cults are also addressed to spirits, which can appear in human or animal shape. The purpose of the festivals of the Melanesians is to renew their vital energy, or **mana**. ☐

The Easter Island statues

From the 9th century, the inhabitants of Easter Island (Rapa Nui in Polynesian) quarried from the walls of the volcano Rano-Raraku enough rock to carve hundreds of moai. These statues stand from 2 to 10 meters (6 to 33 ft.) high and weigh up to 80 tons. They are a type of tiki. The statues either stand alone or in groups in the ahu, sacred precincts that served as temples.

The traditional beliefs of the indigenous peoples living in North and South America are closely connected with nature. The purpose of religious rites was to maintain harmonious relations with the spirits of nature.

The religions of the Na

- **amulet:** an object meant to protect from evil the person who wears it.
- **fast:** abstention from eating for religious reasons.
- **initiation:** a ceremony, sometimes including tests, that marks the acceptance of an individual in a group.
- **myth:** legendary tale that seeks to explain the origin of humankind or of the world.
- **pilgrimage:** a journey that believers make to a holy place for religious reasons.
- **sacrifice:** offering made to a deity, often by killing animals.
- **shaman:** an individual who communicates with the spirits and deities by going into a trance or practicing divination and also uses magical powers to cure the sick.
- **totem:** an animal or plant that a tribe or a clan regards as its ancestor or protector; a representation, usually in the form of a post, of that ancestor.
- **trance:** exalted state of a person transported beyond self and the real world. This state can be achieved by taking substances or by dancing.

The beliefs of the American Indians or Amerindians are closely interwoven with their environment and their way of life. On the plains of North America and in the Amazonian forest, these peoples are traditionally seminomadic hunters and fishers and occasional farmers. In Central America and on the high plateaus of the Andes, people are settled farmers. Since the arrival of Europeans in the 16th century, the religions of their ancestors have been for the Indians a way of affirming and preserving their traditions.

Deities of the North American Indians

The various religions of the North American Indians acknowledge a superior god, the Sky. He is called Chementu (Great Spirit) by the Naskapis of Canada, Nesulk (He-creates-us) by the Micmacs of Newfoundland, or Wakan Tanka (the Great Mysterious One) by the Sioux of the Great Plains. The Great Spirit is

a Navajo shaman creating a sand painting

closely associated with the sun and, when angry, can provoke storms by flashing lightning from his eyes. The Indians are also attached to their foster Mother-Earth, from which they have sprung and which conserves the bones of their ancestors as dust. This attachment to the earth is very strong. For Indians, an individual is nothing who does

Mesa Verde in Colorado was both a fortress-town and a shrine.

totem of the Kwakiutl Indians of Canada

ve Americans

not live on the earth in harmony with the cycles of the universe. This is why hunting peoples felt close to the animals that they hunted and to which they were united by close links or **totems**, usually magical representations of these animals. The animal regarded as the closest to people is the bear, which is human-like in eating everything and walking on its back legs. The Indians call it "cousin" and offer it tobacco. It is a bridge between man and the wilderness. The Navajos venerate Grandmother Spider, the mother of the world, who made man and woman out of a bit of clay. In contrast, other animals are kinds of demons or tricksters. Among these are the coyote, a sort of sorcerer god, which can both cause havoc and repair it, or cause serious illnesses and cure them.

Ever-present gods

Myths recount how the gods taught people to hunt, weave, make baskets or pottery, cultivate corn, and build houses. Therefore, most actions of everyday life are religious: since all these skills were gifts of the gods, people need divine help to practice them. When the Navajos build their hogan, or house, they take care to place it so as not to disturb the spirits. Not all tribes view death in the same way. Indians of the north see it as a natural occurrence, while the Pueblo Indians of the southwestern United States fear the spirits of the dead and must reestablish the harmony that these spirits may destroy. Among the Navajos, a hogan that has contained a corpse must be abandoned.

Rites and practices

As evil and suffering result when the harmony between man and nature is destroyed, it is necessary to reestablish the balance by rites intended to bring about an encounter between humans and spirits. Thus, the rain dance makes it possible for people to commune with the spirits capable of ending drought. For the Pueblo Indians, spirits are present in everyday life. To educate children, they give them dolls called kachinas, which are images of protecting spirits. To enter into contact with the sacred world, the Navajos celebrate "ways," which are rituals that include chants, speeches, and sand paintings.

During **initiation** rites, young people undergo trials that are intended to prove their courage and virility through suffering. Initiates then receive a small leather sack containing remedies and **amulets** to ward off bad luck. **Shamans** claim to be able to cure the gravest illnesses by putting evil spirits to flight. ☐

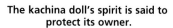

The kachina doll's spirit is said to protect its owner.

The beliefs of the Inuit

The North American people who call themselves Inuit, "human beings," are also known as Eskimos. The Inuit believe that nature is filled with a multitude of spirits, the Inuat, with powers of varying degrees. Aninga, the male spirit of the moon, watches over the earth through a hole he has made in the floor of his house. In the sea, the "Old Woman of the Sea," mistress of the animals, causes hunting to succeed or fail as she pleases. Sila, the Great Spirit, is also master of the winds. Since they live in an icy, hostile world, the Inuit take care not to offend the Inuat, who alone have the power to grant good fishing and hunting. The figure above, which probably represents a spirit, is at the same time man, woman, and bear.

procession during the Pachamama festival

The religions of Latin America

There are Indians in Latin America who still follow rituals inherited from the time of the Incas, before the destruction of the Inca Empire by Europeans in the 16th century. Traditional religions have often become intertwined with Christianity but maintain old characteristics, including the important role given to nature.

Fliers of Mexico

The dramatic pole-flying ceremony, performed near Mexico City, probably has its roots in Aztec custom. Five men climb a pole. One stays at the top, "like the sun," playing music. The others tie ropes to their feet, jump off head first and then circle the pole thirteen times, dangling upside-down.

The Indians of the high plateaus

In the Andes mountains, the festivals and beliefs of the Quechua and Aymara Indians of Peru, Bolivia, and Ecuador are influenced by the ancient cult of the Inca (see p. 29). Thus, in the region of Ayacucho, peasants believe that the quartered body of the long-dead Inca is reconstituting itself and that one day he will come back to drive out the invaders. Many Indians who are now Christians have integrated elements of old beliefs into the new religion. For instance, they believe that during the history of the world there have been many human races, destroyed one after the other by fire, flood, or earthquake. In some regions, the Indians explain that God the Father and Adaneva (Adam and Eve, which they have combined into one person) created the first men. Adaneva fathered a child by the Virgin Mary, a child named Father Manuel or Teete Manuco, who in turn created a new human race and went up to heaven, where he still lives. He dies every year, on Good Friday, but rises from the dead each time. For these

**procession in Peru,
in honor of Manco Capac,
legendary founder of the Inca empire**

traditional dance by Kamayura Indians of Brazil

peoples, who subsist by farming terraced fields on mountainsides, the fruitful earth is vital. They still worship a deity called the Pachamama, whose origins lie far earlier than the Inca empire. Pachamama is the Earth-Mother, who provides food and takes the dead to her bosom. She is the principal divinity of a family of gods of nature and of springs.

Pilgrimages and sacrifices

When they worship the Pachamama in vast pilgrimages, the **Andean** Indians mix the cult of the Earth-Mother with that of the Virgin Mary. They also organize combats in honor of the gods: these can result in deaths, the victims thus becoming **sacrifices**, their blood flowing to feed the divinity. When a new field is first ploughed, it is usual to bury a small slaughtered animal in the soil, so that its blood feeds the Pachamama. The Indians of the high plateaus believe in ghosts and celebrate pagan festivals in honor of the dead on November 2, All Souls' Day in the Christian calendar.

The Indians of the Amazon

Roughly a million and a half Indians, belonging to several hundred tribes, live in the rain forest. They live by hunting and gathering, and they still practice their traditional religions, which include **initiation** rites. To explain the world, they tell stories or **myths**. Some Indians, such as the Tupi-Guaranis, think that supernatural beings created the world, that several human

races have succeeded each other, and that a civilizing hero taught them their skills before withdrawing from the world. They believe that this hero resides in the Land without Evil, a concept similar to the paradise of the Bible. In this paradise, also known as the Land of the Ancestors, corn grows by itself and death is unknown. To glimpse the way to the Land without Evil, shamans go into **trances** and undertake **fasts**. These customs have replaced feasts in which warriors ate parts of the bodies of their enemies to assume their powers. Shamans are also able to interpret omens, signs which tell the will of the gods. □

For the Indians of the equatorial forests of South America, dance has a religious function.

Voodoo mud bath

Voodoo is a religion of Haiti. It emerged from a mixture of African practices and beliefs and Christianity, to which many black Africans brought as slaves to America from the 16th to the 19th centuries were converted. In Haiti, the peasants practice voodoo, which has temples, *houmfos*; priests, *hougans*; and priestesses, *mambos*. The principal deities are *loas*, combinations of Christian saints and African gods. The red-eyed devil is powerful and malevolent. During ceremonies, after the sacrifice of a chicken or an ox, the loas possess believers, who go into trances. Zombies, a type of living dead, can also serve as a link between the world of human beings and the world of the gods.

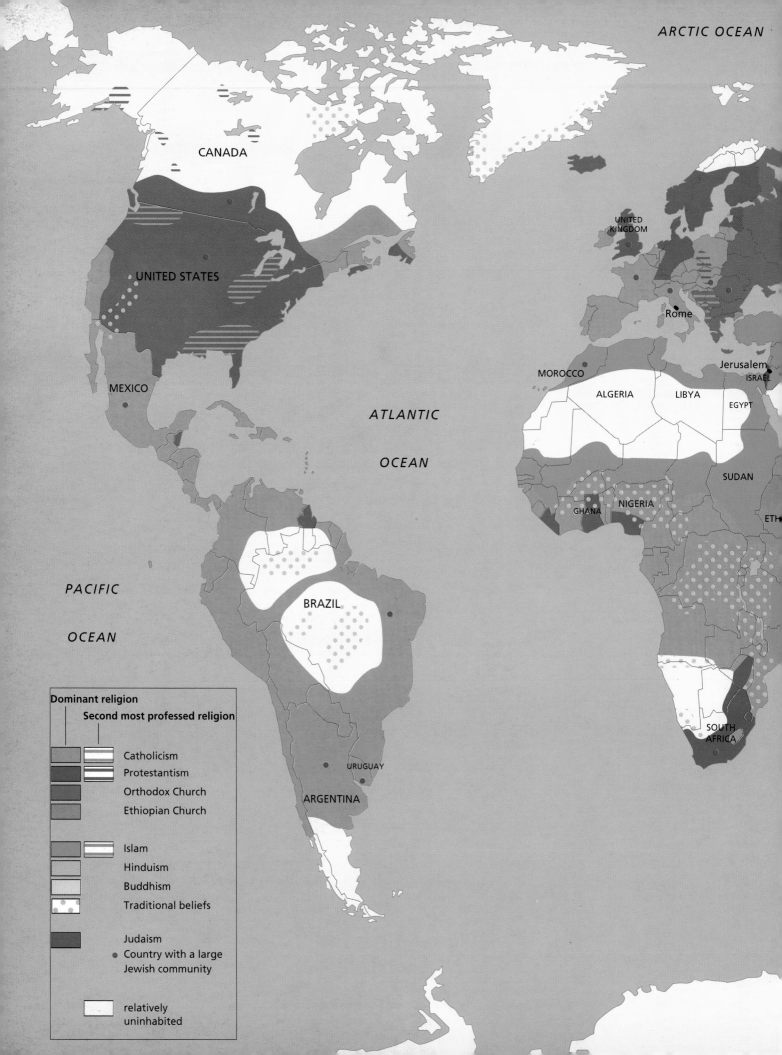

ARCTIC OCEAN

CANADA

UNITED STATES

MEXICO

ATLANTIC

OCEAN

PACIFIC

OCEAN

BRAZIL

URUGUAY

ARGENTINA

UNITED KINGDOM

Rome

MOROCCO

ALGERIA   LIBYA

EGYPT

Jerusalem
ISRAEL

SUDAN

GHANA   NIGERIA

ETH

SOUTH
AFRICA

Dominant religion

Second most professed religion

Catholicism

Protestantism

Orthodox Church

Ethiopian Church

Islam

Hinduism

Buddhism

Traditional beliefs

Judaism
• Country with a large
  Jewish community

relatively
uninhabited

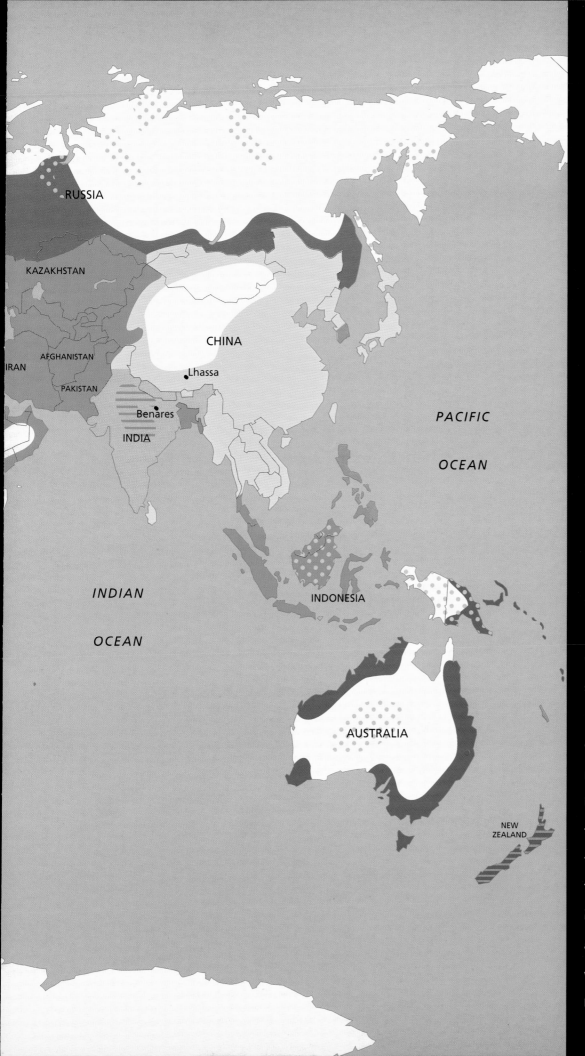

Map of the world's religions

This map shows the current distribution of religions across the world. In each major geographical zone, only the dominant religion and the second most professed religion are shown. In all these zones, however, other religions not represented on the map may be practiced by communities of various sizes. The map was drawn on the basis of the number of persons declaring membership of a religion, even if they did not practice it regularly: thus, since 85 percent of French people declare themselves Catholics, Catholicism is shown as the dominant religion in France, although only 10 percent in fact practice their religion. Lastly, it is often difficult to assess the number of persons following traditional beliefs. Therefore, these may be underrepresented in the map although such beliefs are still widely followed in Africa, Latin America, and Oceania.

?

Did you know?

Where does the word *religion* come from?

Experts cannot agree. Some specialists think that the word comes from the Latin verb *relegere*, which means "to assemble scrupulously," since those who concerned themselves with the cult of the gods took great care in doing so. Others believe that the word is derived from the Latin *religare*, "to tie," since religion is what binds man to the supernatural. In fact, in ancient times there was no specific word to describe religion, since it played a part in all the activities of everyday life.

What is fundamentalism?

Fundamentalists are followers of a religion who decide to practice all rules and rites by returning to initial practices without considering how they have changed over time. At the beginning of the 20th century, a fundamentalist current opposing any modernization arose within the Catholic Church. In the Muslim world, the aim of fundamentalist movements is that the prescriptions imposed by the Koran and by tradition be fully applied to the whole of society.

Is Jesus Christ an important figure for the Muslims?

Yes. Jesus is mentioned thirty-five times in the Koran, the sacred book of the Muslims. At some points he is referred to as Iesa Ibn Maryam, "Jesus, son of Mary," and in other places as the Messiah. Like the Christians, Muslims think that Jesus was sent by God, but they do not regard him as the son of God and do not heed his call to change the world. According to the Koran, Jesus is simply a prophet, who proclaimed the coming of Mohammed, and Mariam, his mother, the Virgin Mary of Christians, is a holy woman.

Are there points in common between Greco-Roman beliefs and Hinduism?

The Indians, the Greeks, and Romans, as well as the Iranian and Germanic peoples, are all Indo-Europeans. Their languages have a common origin, and their beliefs are based around three principal gods: a creator god (Zeus, Jupiter, Brahma . . .), a warrior god, and a civilizer-cultivator. These categories corresponded to ancient societies that were divided between those who prayed (priests), those who fought (warriors), and those who worked (artisans and peasants).

Is the pope a head of state?

Yes. He rules over Vatican City, one of the smallest states in world. Until the 19th century, the Pope wielded two kinds of power: spiritual power, of a religious nature, and temporal power, of a political nature. The Papal States, which varied in size over the centuries, included the city of Rome and the surrounding regions of Italy. In 1870, the King of Italy (Victor Emmanuel II) made Rome his capital, and the pope thus lost his temporal power. However, in 1929, an agreement was concluded with the Italian state, which recognized Vatican City as an independent state in the heart of Rome, with its own courts, police, press, postal service, and ambassadors. However, the authority of the pope today is above all spiritual and moral.

Why does the snake play different roles in several religions?

Snakes can be poisonous, and they can move without arms or legs, crawling along the ground, climbing trees, and swimming. In many religions, the snake is portrayed as an artful creature, a link between the powers of the fruitful earth and the powers of the sky, which holds the sun, also a source of life. Because snakes were often feared, the snake came to symbolize evil, as in the story of Adam and Eve and in the myths of Mesopotamia, where it is defeated by the god Marduk. The snake can also be beneficial to humans, like the snake coiled around the cadeus, the staff borne by Asclepius, the Greek healer-god.

In which countries are the Muslims the most numerous?

Contrary to what is often assumed, all Muslims are not Arabs and all Arabs are not Muslims. In total there are about 1 billion Muslims, of whom only 200 million are Arabs.

Ten million Arabs are Christians. In Indonesia, an island group with 180 million inhabitants, 43 percent of the population are Muslims; Pakistan (98 million inhabitants) and Bangladesh (100 million inhabitants) are around 90 percent Muslim.

What is a saint?

The original meaning of this word was "venerated." The first Christians started the custom of adding it to the name of believers who had lived a life that most closely conformed with the teachings of the Gospels. Catholics believe that saints can intervene with God and celebrate ceremonies in their honor. The majority of Protestants reject the cult of the saints, and some also dislike the custom of representing saints in statues and paintings. The word *saint* also describes persons of exemplary behavior such as the Muslim marabouts, saintly hermits whose tombs are the focus of pilgrimages.

What is mysticism?

In all religions, men and women "thirsting for God" try to come closer to the supernatural. This they achieve in particular through prayer and meditation. Thus they can reach a special state during which so-called abnormal phenomena, such as levitation (floating in the air) or visions occur.

What is the cargo cult?

Since the end of the 19th century, in some of the islands of Melanesia, the Kago or cargo cult has been practiced. In the Solomon Islands and in Papua New Guinea, the followers of this cult await an extraordinary boat that, according to their prophets, will bring their ancestors with a cargo of tools and seeds. This cargo will enable people to plant vegetable gardens and produce everything they need without having to work. The fabulous cargo ship will take the whites (European settlers) back to their homes. Experts think that these beliefs date from the time when the Melanesians first saw the arrival of ships bringing Europeans, who then proceeded to take control of their islands by force.

What is the difference between Israelite and Israeli?

The children of Israel, another name of Jacob, the son of Isaac and grandson of Abraham, are called Israelites. This is one of the names of the Jewish people, known as the "Hebrews" in former times. The Israelis are the citizens of the state of Israel, established in 1948. Jews who do not live in Israel are Israelites, but they are not Israelis.

What is kathakali?

Kathakali is a form of theater that is widespread in India. Performances enact stories taken from the great Indian epics, the Ramayana and Mahabharata. The actors all are men and wear brightly colored costumes. Their faces are made up to look like masks, and the actors' expressions and gestures are determined by ancient rules.

In what way are some expressions linked to religion?

There are a number of expressions that are derived from the Bible or from Greek and Roman mythology. For instance, to speak of "a paradise on earth" or "Eden" is to mean a place of perfect beauty, like the Garden of Eden, described in the Bible as an earthly paradise. A woman can be described as "beautiful as Venus," the Roman goddess of love; an "Apollo" is an exceptionally handsome man— Apollo being the Greek and Roman god of the sun and the arts, the most handsome of the gods. Someone said to be "as strong as Hercules" is being likened to the Greek hero who accomplished twelve tasks considered impossible without superhuman strength.

Zeus

Cernunnos

Ganesha

Demeter

The Gods

☽ Mesopotamia

Adad: god of tempests and storms. Symbol: lightning.

An (or Anu): creator of the universe, father of the gods and god of the sky. His symbol is a horned headdress.

Enki or Ea: god of water, wisdom, and magic, symbolized by a fish.

Enlil: son of An and lord of the universe. He is symbolized by a horned headdress.

Inanna-Ishtar: goddess of fertility, love, and war, symbolized by a star.

Marduk: from the second millennium B.C. considered the father of the gods.

Ninurta: god of war, hunting, and hurricanes, represented by a scepter decorated with two lion heads.

Shamash: god of the sun and of justice, whose symbol is the solar disc.

Sin: god of the moon, symbolized by a crescent.

☽ Egypt

In different cities of ancient Egypt, people worshiped gods under various names and appearances but with similar attributes.

Amun: god of the beneficial sun, the most important of the gods. Honored in the city of **92** Thebes, where he was

represented with the head of a ram, or as a man wearing a feathered headdress.

Anubis: the jackal-headed god of embalmers.

Apis: god of Memphis, associated with Ptah in a fertility cult, and represented by a white bull with black marks.

Bes: an ugly but helpful god, represented as a grotesque gnome.

Hathor: goddess of the sky, joy, and love, at times represented as a cow.

Horus: son of Isis and Osiris, the hawk-headed patron god of Egypt.

Isis: goddess of magic and life, wife and sister of Osiris, depicted as a woman.

Maat: goddess of justice, depicted as a woman with an ostrich plume.

Osiris: god of death and vegetation, who wears the white headgear of the pharaohs. He is often depicted with a greenish color for he is not quite alive.

Re (Ra): a sun god, who was later combined with Amun, and represented as a man or as a falcon.

Seth: brother of Osiris, a malevolent god who is lord of the desert, and is sometimes depicted as a hare with a forked tail and a long muzzle.

Thoth: god of numbers,

inventor of writing, is depicted as an ibis-headed man or a baboon.

☽ Greece

This list includes only the principal Greek gods. They were subsequently adopted by the Romans, who gave them different names.

Aphrodite (Roman Venus): goddess of love and pleasure, depicted as a beautiful young woman, accompanied by her son Eros (symbolizing Love), a child armed with a bow.

Apollo (Apollo in Rome): son of Zeus, god of the sun and the arts, often depicted as a handsome young man holding a lyre or driving the chariot of the sun.

Ares (Roman Mars): son of Zeus and Hera, the god of war, irascible, and often depicted as an armored warrior.

Artemis (Roman Diana): the sister of Apollo, goddess of the moon and hunting and patroness of young girls; depicted as a huntress, with a crescent moon in her hair.

Asclepius (Roman Aesculapius): the son of Apollo, the healing god to whom there was a major cult in Epidaurus. He carries a stick or staff around that twines a snake.

Athena (Roman Minerva): goddess of wisdom, arts, and sciences, and patron of Athens, who sprang fully armed from the head of Zeus. She is depicted helmeted and carrying a spear and shield. Her emblem is the owl.

Cronos (Roman Saturn): the god of time and destiny; father of Zeus.

Demeter (Roman Ceres): sister of Zeus, goddess of the harvests, and often depicted crowned with ears of wheat. For four months of the year, she cannot see her daughter, Koré, who reigns in the Underworld under the name of Persephone (Roman Proserpina); she leaves the underworld only for the sowing.

Dionysus (Roman Bacchus): god of vegetation, wine, and drunkenness; depicted crowned with a vine branch with clusters of grapes.

Hades (Roman Pluto): god of the underworld and of death, brother of Zeus; he is rarely depicted, for he inspires fear.

Hephaestos (Roman Vulcan): god of artisans and in particular blacksmiths; uncouth, lame, and ugly, he is the jealous husband of Aphrodite.

Hera: (Roman Juno): wife and sister of Zeus, the guardian of marriage.

Rê

Vishnou

Inanna-Ishtar

Kali

Hermes (Roman Mercury): son of Zeus and god of trickery, travelers, and trade. The messenger of the gods, he wears a round hat adorned with feathers, and winged sandals.

Hestia (Roman Vesta): goddess of the hearth and sister of Zeus, guardian of the home.

Poseidon (Roman Neptune): brother of Zeus and god of the sea, he is usually shown holding a trident.

Zeus (Roman Jupiter): ruler of the gods, god of the sky and storms, he is usually depicted bearded and wielding a thunderbolt.

❶ Rome

When the Romans first came into contact with Greek culture they adopted their gods, sometimes giving them different powers and attributes. They also continued to worship their old Roman gods.

Janus: old Roman god, the god of beginnings and endings. He has two faces.

Juno: goddess of childbirth, and guardian of every woman (Greek Hera).

Jupiter: in addition to the roles of Zeus, the guardian of the city of Rome.

Mars: god of war, who is more important than Ares is for the

Greeks; he also plays a role in agriculture. He is married to Bellona, the goddess of war.

Saturn: god of vine growers and peasants. The original Roman god was identified with Cronos. He is depicted as an old man, naked or in a cloak.

Vesta: the most beautiful and respected Roman goddess is symbolized by pure flame.

❶ Celtic regions

The gods of the Celts of Britain, Ireland, or Gaul are basically the same under different names. When the Romans conquered Gaul and Britain, the Celtic gods were assimilated into the Roman gods.

Belenus (Gaul): god of light.

Borvo (Gaul): healer god, assimilated to Apollo.

Cernunnos (Gaul): antlered god, and lord of the animals.

Epona (Gaul) or Brigit (Ireland): the "shining one," daughter of Dagda and mother of the other gods; the mounted goddess of war and wisdom.

Esus: a warrior god, and the largest of the gods; inventor of all the arts. He was assimilated to Mercury.

Lug: the supreme god; the god of arts and skills.

Ogmios (Gaul), Ogme or Elcmar (Ireland): god of ingenuity and eloquence.

Taranis (Gaul) or Dagda (Ireland): god of light, air, life, and death. Assimilated to Jupiter, he carries a club, a symbol of power; a cauldron, a symbol of abundance; and a wheel, representing the universe.

Teutates (or Toutatis): god of the tribes and god of war. Later assimilated to the god Mars.

❶ India

Since the second millennium B.C., Hinduism has evolved. Hindus still believed in the older gods (such as Indra, Agni, and Brahma), but they began to prefer other more popular gods such as Shiva and Vishnu.

Agni: very ancient god of fire, work, and fertility.

Brahma: the creator god, often depicted as pink, with four faces and four arms, mounted on a wild duck or on a swan.

Ganesha: son of Shiva, and god of arts, sciences, and trades. He has an elephant's head, an obese body, and rides on a rat.

Indra: god of creative energy, war, and victory. He rides an elephant and is armed with lightning. He is later combined with Vishnu.

Kali: "Black One," wife of Shiva. Another name of the goddess Parvati ("Mountain Dweller"), the ten-armed goddess of war.

Krishna: benevolent reincarnation of Vishnu and deliverer from tyrants. He is depicted as a baby dancing on the serpent that he has tamed. He has been the subject of a major cult, at times in association with his wife, Rada.

Lakshmi: "Splendor," the wife of Vishnu.

Mitra-Varuna: Pairing of Day and Night, among the most ancient gods.

Shiva: both beneficial and destructive, depicted as a god of dancing, with a necklace of skulls. He is shown with three eyes and four arms and is usually dark blue. He rides on a white bull or an eagle.

Surya: an ancient god of the sun, god of descent and living beings, he is usually dark red with three eyes and four arms and seated on a lotus. He was later assimilated to Brahma.

Vishnu: "the Penetrating," the beneficial creator and savior. He has been reincarnated more then ten times. Often depicted in dark-blue, he rides a white elephant or an eagle.

Index

Crédits photographiques

Couverture : Launois J. – Rapho. *Peinture murale dans une église orthodoxe bulgare* ; Sitton H. – Fotogram-Stone. *Grand stupa de Bodnath, Népal* ; Josse H. *Site de Delphes, Grèce* ; Josse H. *Juifs devant le Mur occidental, Jérusalem* ; Dagli Orti G. *« Vie de la Vierge et du Christ : la Cène », Giotto* ; chapelle Scrovegni, Padoue ; Michaud R. et S. – Rapho. *Prière au coucher du soleil.*
Dos de couverture : VCL – Pix. *Mosquée d'Ispahan, Iran*
Pages de garde : Held S.
Page titre : Kunsthistorisches Museum, Vienne. *Dionysos et Héphaistos.*

p. 2-hg   Kirtley M. et A. – ANA. *Maquillage de cérémonie, tribu Dam, Côte d'Ivoire.*
p. 2-bd   Duchêne J.P. – Diaf. *Lecteur de Coran*
p. 3-m   Josse H., *Chemin du mort dans l'au-delà égyptien, Musée du Louvre, Paris.*
p. 4-hg   Bridgeman Art Library – Giraudon. *Pesée de l'âme ; British Museum, Londres.*
p. 4-mh   Gruyaert H. – Magnum.
p. 4-hd   Explorer.
p. 4-mg   Josse H. *Musée du Louvre, Paris.*
p. 4-mbg   Kunsthistorisches Museum, Vienne.
p. 4-b   Dagli Orti G. *Mosquée d'Omar, Jérusalem.*
p. 4-mhd   Spiegel T. – Rapho.
p. 4-mmd   De Soye J.N. – Rapho.
p. 4-mbd   Abbas – Magnum.
p. 5-mh   Mayer F. – Magnum.
p. 5-hd   Martel O. – Icône.
p. 5-mhg   Michaud R. et S. – Rapho.
p. 5-mbg   Martin D.
p. 5-mhd   Friedel M. – Rapho.
p. 5-bg   Riffet – Explorer.
p. 5-bg   Mauger Th. – Explorer. *Sadduh, Rajasthan.*
p. 5-bd   Hoa-Qui. *Moine bouddhiste, Thaïlande.*
p. 6-g   Held A. – Artephot. *St Simon le Stylite, icône grecque, 1664 ; M.A.H., Genève.*
p. 6-b   Held S.
p. 7-h   Burri R. – Magnum.
p. 7-mg   Michaud R. et S. – Rapho.
p. 7-md   Woodfin Camp / Garrett K. – Cosmos.
p. 7-bd   Lauros – Giraudon. *« Miroir de l'humaine salvation », école flamande, XV s. ; musée Condé, Chantilly.*
p. 8-hg   Lessing E. – Magnum. *Porteur d'offrandes de Tello, Mésopotamie ; musée du Louvre, Paris.*
p. 8-h   Burri R. – Magnum. *Mains négatives dans la grotte de Perito Moreno, Argentine.*
p. 8-mg   Bridgeman Art Library, – Giraudon. *Pesée de l'âme ; British Museum, Londres.*
p. 8-mb   Josse H. *Site de Delphes, Grèce.*
p. 8-b   Dagli Orti G. *Animaux fantastiques celtes ; Musée national, Copenhague.*
p. 9-hd   Dagli Orti G. *Musée national d'archéologie, Lima.*
p. 9-b   Dagli Orti G. *Zeus, Ganymède et Hestia ; Musée de Tarquinia.*
p. 10-hg   Ducasse F. – Rapho. *Dolmens.*
p. 10-b   Réunion des musées nationaux, Paris. *musée des Antiquités nationales, St-Germain-en-Laye.*
p. 11-h   Burri R. – Magnum.
p. 11-g   Dagli Orti G.
p. 11-d   Gerster G. – Rapho.
p. 11-b   Dagli Orti G. *Musée hittite, Ankara.*
p. 12-hg   Gerster G. – Rapho. *Ziggourat d'Our (Iraq).*
p. 12-b   Dagli Orti G. *Musée de Bagdad, Iraq.*
p. 13-h   Lessing E. – Magnum. *Vorderasiatisches Museum, Berlin.*
p. 13-g   Dagli Orti G. *Musée archéologique d'Alep, Syrie.*
p. 13-d   Dagli Orti G. *Musée du Louvre, Paris.*
p. 13-b   Dagli Orti G. *Musée archéologique d'Alep, Syrie.*
p. 14-hg   Josse H. *Grand sphinx, musée du Louvre, Paris.*
p. 14-b   Lessing E. – Magnum. *« Triade d'Osorkon », XVII dynastie ; musée du Louvre, Paris.*
p. 15-h   Lessing E. – Magnum. *« Livre des morts » de Neqbed ; chapelle blanche, Karnak, Luxor.*
p. 15-g   Dagli Orti G. *Stèle de la Dame de Taperet, XXII dynastie ; musée du Louvre, Paris.*
p. 15-d   Dagli Orti G. *Musée du Louvre, Paris.*
p. 15-b   Josse H. *Musée du Louvre, Paris.*
p. 16-h   Josse H. *« Livre des morts » de Neqbed ; musée du Louvre, Paris.*
p. 16-d   Dagli Orti G. *Barque prov. du trésor de Toutankhamon ; Musée égyptien, Le Caire.*
p. 16-b   Dagli Orti G. *Musée du Louvre, Paris.*
p. 17-h   Josse H. *Musée du Louvre, Paris.*
p. 17-b   Ross J.G. – Rapho.
p. 17-d   Dagli Orti G. *Vase canope de la tombe de Kha.*
p. 18/19   Giraudon. *Musée du Louvre, Paris.*
p. 19-hd   Bridgeman Art Library – Giraudon. *Pesée de l'âme ; British Museum, Londres.*
p. 20-hg   Réunion des musées nationaux, Paris. *Ganymède, musée du Louvre, Paris.*
p. 20-b   Dagli Orti G.
p. 21-h   Kunsthistorisches Museum, Vienne.
p. 21-m1   Dagli Orti G. *Musée national, Athènes.*
p. 21-m2   Dagli Orti G. *Musée archéologique Guelma, Algérie.*
p. 21-m3   Dagli Orti G. *Musée national d'Archéologie, Athènes.*
p. 21-m4   Nimatallah – Artephot.

p. 21-m5   Dagli Orti G. *Musée de l'Acropole, Athènes.*
p. 21-m6   Josse H. *Musée du Louvre, Paris.*
p. 21-m7   Josse H. *Musée de Delphes, Grèce.*
p. 21-m8   Dagli Orti G. *Musée archéologique de l'île de Thassos, Grèce.*
p. 21-m9   Dagli Orti G. *Antiquarium de Metaponto, Italie.*
p. 21-m10   Dagli Orti G. *Musée archéologique, Venise.*
p. 21-m11   Josse H. *Musée du Louvre, Paris.*
p. 21-m12   Dagli Orti G. *Musée archéologique, Le Pirée, Athènes.*
p. 21-md   Dagli Orti G. *Musée national, Athènes.*
p. 21-bd   Josse H. *Musée du Louvre, Paris.*
p. 22-h   Josse H.
p. 22-hg   Bildarchiv – Artephot. *Antikenmuseum Staatliches Museen Preuss Kulturbesitz, Berlin.*
p. 22-b   Dagli Orti G. *Musée national d'Archéologie, Tarente.*
p. 23-h   Dagli Orti G.
p. 23-g   Dagli Orti G. *Villa Giulia, Rome.*
p. 23-d   Dagli Orti G. *Musée du Louvre, Paris.*
p. 23-b   Dagli Orti G. *Villa Giulia, Rome.*
p. 24-hg   Dagli Orti G. *Poséidon et Amphitrite ; Musée archéologique, Naples.*
p. 24-d   Dagli Orti G.
p. 25-h   Dagli Orti G. *Maison du Ménandre, Pompéi.*
p. 25-m   Dagli Orti G. *Musée de la civilisation romaine, Rome.*
p. 25-b   Josse H. *« Sarcophage des époux », VI s. av. J.-C. ; musée du Louvre, Paris.*
p. 26-h   Lessing E. – Magnum. *Porte d'un sanctuaire celto-ligurien ; musée Borély, Marseille.*
p. 26-b   Dagli Orti G. *Musée des Antiquités nationales, St-Germain-en-Laye.*
p. 27-h   Dagli Orti G. *Chaudron de Gündestrup ; Musée national, Copenhague.*
p. 27-m   Werner Forman Archive. *Musée national, Reykjavik.*
p. 27-b   Lessing E. – Magnum.
p. 28-hg   Dagli Orti G. *Naissance de Quetzacóatl ; Musée national d'anthropologie, Mexico.*
p. 28-b   Dagli Orti G. *Musée national d'archéologie, Guatemala.*
p. 29-h   Dagli Orti G. *« Codex Borbonicus » ; Bibliothèque du Palais Bourbon, Paris.*
p. 29-md   Vautier M. – ANA. *« Codex Florentino » ; Antochiw Collection.*
p. 29-b   Dagli Orti G.
p. 30-h   Dagli Orti G. *« La Cène », P. Lorenzetti ; Basilique St-François, Assise.*
p. 30-h   Hayaux du Tilly M. *Désert de Juda, Judée.*
p. 30-mh   Spiegel T. – Rapho. *Juifs devant le Mur occidental, Jérusalem.*
p. 30-mh   Ducasse F. – Rapho. *Communion solennelle.*
p. 30-b   Abbas – Magnum. *Pèlerins autour de la Kaaba pour la prière du soir, La Mecque.*
p. 31-h   Explorer. *Juif lisant la Bible sous un dais.*
p. 31-b   Dagli Orti G. *Mosquée d'Omar, Jérusalem.*
p. 32-hg   Michaud R. et S. – Rapho. *Ange Gabriel extrait du « Livre des Merveilles » (Iraq) ; Bibliothèque de Munich, Allemagne.*
p. 32-b   Radovan Z. *Musée d'Israël, Jérusalem.*
p. 33-h   Hayaux du Tilly M.
p. 33-m   Michaud R. et S. – Rapho.
p. 33-hd   Josse H. *« Dyptique de la Tentation : le péché », Hugo Van der Goes, 1664.*
p. 33-bd   Dagli Orti G. *Miniature extraite du « Falmane », 1610 ; musée Topkapi, Istanbul.*
p. 34-hg   Hayaux du Tilly M. *Étoile de David à 6 branches (megen David) ; Capharnaüm, Israël.*
p. 34-m   Radovan Z. *Musée d'Israël, Jérusalem.*
p. 35-h   Lessing E. – Magnum. *« Le Triomphe de Titus » ; Forum, Rome.*
p. 35-h   CIRIC.
p. 35-hd   Dagli Orti G. *Bibliothèque nationale, Lisbonne.*
p. 36-h   Spiegel T. – Rapho.
p. 36-hg   Phedon Salou – Artephot. *Collection Institut catholique, Paris.*
p. 36-h   Nowitz R. – Explorer.
p. 37-h   Gruyaert H. – Magnum.
p. 37-m   Dagli Orti G. *Bibliothèque nationale, Lisbonne.*
p. 37-bd   Spiegel T. – Rapho.
p. 38-b   Spiegel T. – Rapho.
p. 38-h   Spiegel T. – Rapho.
p. 38-b   Mayer F. – Magnum.
p. 39-h   Searle B. – Halliday S. and Lushington L.
p. 39-m   Martel O. – Explorer.
p. 39-bd   Lissac P. – Explorer.
p. 40-hg   Dagli Orti G. *Christ bénissant, cathédrale Ste-Sophie, Istanbul.*
p. 40-h   Dagli Orti G. *« Vie de la Vierge et du Christ : la crucifixion », Giotto, 1303-1305 ; chapelle Scrovegni, Padoue.*
p. 41-h   Dagli Orti G. *« Vie de la Vierge et du Christ : la Cène », Giotto, 1303-1305 ; chapelle Scrovegni, Padoue.*
p. 41-m   Dagli Orti G. *« La Nativité », Fra Angelico ; couvent St-Marc, Florence.*
p. 41-b   Alinari – Giraudon. *« Vie de la Vierge et Christ : la résurrection », Giotto, 1303-1305 ; chapelle Scrovegni, Padoue.*

p. 41-hd   Dagli Orti G. *Musée d'art chrétien, Carthage.*
p. 41-bd   Held A. – Artephot. *Musée du Louvre, Paris.*
p. 42-h   Mazin R. *Église de Germigny-des-Prés, Loiret.*
p. 42-m   Bibliothèque Apostolique, Vatican.
p. 42-bø   Held A. – Artephot. *Catacombes de Priscilla, Rome.*
p. 43-h   Dagli Orti G. *« Vie de la Vierge et du Christ : le baptême de Jésus », Giotto, 1303-1305 ; chapelle Scrovegni, Padoue.*
p. 43-hd   Dagli Orti G. *Musée du Bardo, Tunis.*
p. 43-bd   Coll. Larousse. *Bibliothèque nationale, Paris.*
p. 44-h   Josse H. *Extrait des « Chroniques » de David Aubert, XV s. ; Bibliothèque de l'Arsenal, Paris.*
p. 44-bg   Dagli Orti G. *« St Dominique et les Albigeois », P. Berruguete, fin XV s. ; musée du Prado, Madrid.*
p. 45-h   Dagli Orti G. *« Concile de Trente », fresque des frères Zuccari, 1560-1566 ; palais Farnèse, Caprarola.*
p. 45-m   Sudres J.D. – Scope. *Cathédrale St Lizier, Limoges.*
p. 45-bg   AKG, Berlin. *« Luther, Érasme et les Réformateurs », copie de L. Cranach, XV s. ; salle de Luther, Wittenberg.*
p. 45-md   Josse H. *Musée Boymans, Pays-Bas.*
p. 46-h   Gorianov A. – ANA.
p. 46-b   Launois J. – Rapho.
p. 46-hg   Bonnefoy – Top. *« Trinité », A. Roublev ; galerie Tretiakov, Moscou.*
p. 46-bg   Coll. Larousse. *Vierge de Vladimir, icône byzantine, XII s.*
p. 47-h   Martel O. – Icône.
p. 47-m   Sioen G. – Rapho.
p. 47-d   Gérard B. – Explorer.
p. 48-h   Black Star/Turnley D. – Rapho.
p. 48-b   Testut A. – Rapho.
p. 48-hg   Ansin – Gamma.
p. 49-h   Woodfin Camp and Associates/Akhtar H. – Cosmos.
p. 49-h   Peress S. – Magnum.
p. 49-d   Black Star/Schulke F. – Rapho.
p. 50-h   Explorer.
p. 50-bd   Dannic – Diaf.
p. 50-hg   Pinoges A. – CIRIC.
p. 50-g   Luider E. – Rapho.
p. 51-h   De Soye J.N. – Rapho.
p. 51-h   Setbon M.-Black Star – Rapho.
p. 51-b   Pinoges A. – CIRIC.
p. 52/53   Stone S. – Fotogram-Stone.
p. 53-h   Dagli Orti G. *Sacrifice d'Abraham ; église San Vitale, Ravenne.*
p. 54-hg   Michaud R. et S. – Rapho. *Syllabe sacrée signifiant Allah.*
p. 54-m   Coll. Larousse. *Bibliothèque nationale, Paris.*
p. 55-h   Coll. Larousse. *Bibliothèque nationale, Paris.*
p. 55-b   Henri Stierling.
p. 56-h   Michaud R. et S. – Rapho.
p. 56-m   Mandel G. – Artephot. *Miniature persane, XVIII s. ; collection Medicea di Fiazole, Florence.*
p. 56-m   Dagli Orti G. *Musée islamique, Le Caire.*
p. 57-h   Mazin R.
p. 57-d   Abbas – Magnum.
p. 58-h   Abbas – Magnum.
p. 58-m   Michaud R. et S. – Rapho.
p. 58-b   Frerck R./Odyssey/Chicago – Cosmos.
p. 59-h   Michaud R. et S. – Rapho.
p. 59-d   Michaud R. et S. – Rapho.
p. 59-b   Abbas – Magnum.
p. 60-h   Held S. *Brahmane lisant des textes sacrés.*
p. 60-h   Michaud R.et S. – Rapho. *Krishna et Radha.*
p. 60-mh   Michaud R. et S. – Rapho. *Offrande de lait à Bahubali.*
p. 60-mb   Martin A. *Moulins à prières bouddhiques.*
p. 60-b   Koch P. – Rapho. *Sanctuaire naturel shinto (Miyajima, Japon).*
p. 61-hd   Michaud R. et S. – Rapho. *Symbole du Yin et du Yang.*
p. 61-b   Held S. *Grand Bouddha Kama Kura, Japon.*
p. 62-hg   Michaud R. et S. – Rapho. *Syllabe sacrée hindoue « aum ».*
p. 62-mg   Michaud R. et S. – Rapho.
p. 62-md   Michaud R. et S. – Rapho.
p. 63-h   Werner Forman Archive. *Galerie nationale, Prague.*
p. 63-b   Held S.
p. 63-d   Held S.
p. 64-h   Hoepker T. – Magnum.
p. 64-b   Michaud R. et S. – Rapho.
p. 64-g   Held S.
p. 65-h   Michaud R. et S. – Rapho.
p. 65-m   Held S.
p. 65-hd   Barbey B. – Magnum.
p. 65-bd   Explorer.
p. 66-hg   De Wilde P. – Hoa-Qui. *Jaïn.*
p. 66-h   De Wilde P. – Hoa-Qui.
p. 67-h   De Wilde P. – Hoa-Qui.
p. 67-hd   Barbelette E. – Magnum.

p. 67-bd   Rai R. – Magnum.
p. 68-hg   Dugast J.L. – Hoa-Qui.
p. 68-h   Held S.
p. 69-h   Held S.
p. 69-m   Nou J.L.
p. 69-d   Michaud R. et S. – Rapho.
p. 70-h   De Wilde P. – Hoa-Qui.
p. 70-hg   Held S.
p. 70-hg   Martin A.
p. 70-b   Held S.
p. 71-h   Charbonneau J.,
p. 71-m   Michaud R. et S. – Rapho.
p. 71-d   Held S.
p. 72/73   Rebmann L. – Explorer.
p. 73-hd   Nou J.L. – Explorer. *Nirvana du Bouddha.*
p. 74-h   Michaud R. et S. – Rapho. *Symbole du Yin et du Yang.*
p. 74-mg   Michaud R. et S. – Rapho. *Collection privée.*
p. 74-b   Michaud R. et S. – Rapho.
p. 75-h   Riboud M. – Magnum.
p. 75-mg   Henriette C. – Icône.
p. 75-md   Mayer F. – Magnum.
p. 75-bd   Michaud R. et S. – Rapho. *Collection privée.*
p. 76-hg   Boisvieux C. *Torii du sanctuaire Inari de Tsuwano, Japon.*
p. 76-h   Boisvieux C.
p. 77-h   Haas – Magnum.
p. 77-b   Silvester H. – Rapho.
p. 77-h   Hoepker T. – Magnum.
p. 77-bd   Koch P. – Rapho.
p. 78-hc   Maxima/Hattenb – Hoa-Qui. *Totem, Indiens Kwakiutl, Canada.*
p. 78-h   Martel O. – Icône. *Fête des féticheuses, Côte d'Ivoire.*
p. 78-mh   De Wilde P. – Hoa-Qui. *Papou de Nouvelle-Guinée.*
p. 78-mb   Lénars C. *Peinture sacrée navajo sur sable.*
p. 78-b   Charliat – Rapho. *Fête des Masques, lac Titicaca (Pérou).*
p. 79-hd   Destable D. – Musée de l'Homme, Paris. *Tiki polynésien.*
p. 79-b   De Hogues B. – Fotogram-Stone. *Danseurs Intore, Burundi.*
p. 80-hg   Kirtley M. et A. – ANA. *Maquillage de cérémonie, tribu Dam, Côte d'Ivoire.*
p. 80-b   Johns C. – Fotogram-Stone.
p. 81-h   Martel O. – Icône.
p. 81-hd   Held S. *Musée d'Abidjan, Côte d'Ivoire.*
p. 81-bd   Oster J. – Musée de l'Homme, Paris.
p. 81-m   Renaudeau M. – Hoa-Qui.
p. 82-h   Valentin D. – Hoa-Qui. *Mont Ayers Rock.*
p. 82-m   Lewandowski H. – Réunion des Musées Nationaux, Paris. *Musée des Arts africains et océaniens, Paris.*
p. 83-h   De Wilde P. – Hoa-Qui.
p. 83-m   Ponsard D. – Musée de l'Homme, Paris.
p. 83-bd   Martin A.
p. 84-h   Lénars C. *Peinture hopie.*
p. 84-m   Lénars C.
p. 84-b   Lénars C.
p. 85-h   Koch P. – Rapho.
p. 85-b   Musée de l'Homme, Paris.
p. 85-d   Destable D. – Musée de l'Homme, Paris.
p. 86-h   Lainé D. – Cosmos.
p. 86-g   Vautier M. – ANA.
p. 86-b   Lainé D. – Cosmos.
p. 87-h   Friedel M. – Rapho.
p. 87-d   Steber M. – Cosmos.
p. 87-b   JB Pictures/Perry S. – Cosmos.
p. 90-h   Michaud R. et S. – Rapho.
p. 90-mh   Giraudon. *Hôtel Ratlé, Fribourg.*
p. 90-hd   Josse H. *Musée des Beaux-Arts, Rouen.*
p. 90-bg   Michaud R. et S. – Rapho.
p. 91-hg   Josse H. *Église St-Sulpice, Paris.*
p. 91-mhg   Michaud R. et S. – Rapho.
p. 91-mhd   Le Diascorn F. – Rapho.
p. 91-mhd   Coll. Larousse. *Bibliothèque nationale, Paris.*
p. 92-hg   Dagli Orti G. *Musée Nicosie, Chypre.*
p. 92-mhg   Lessing E. – Magnum. *Musée national, Copenhague.*
p. 92-mhd   Michaud R. et S. – Rapho. *Collection privée.*
p. 92-hd   Dagli Orti G. *Musée archéologique, Syracuse.*
p. 93-h   Dagli Orti G. *Musée du Louvre, Paris.*
p. 93-mhg   Michaud R. et S. – Rapho. *Collection privée.*
p. 93-mhd   Giraudon. *Musée national, Damas.*
p. 93-hd   Michaud R. et S. – Rapho. *Collection privée.*

Cartes pp. 13, 15, 21, 25, 27, 29, 35, 55 : Graffito

Carte p. 88-89 : préparation et réalisation : Krystyna Mazoyer-Dzieniszewska
mise en couleur : Léonie Schlosser

Photogravure : Arrigo, Bordeaux - Mame Imprimeurs, Tours - Dépôt légal septembre 1995 - N° de série éditeur : 19332
Imprimé en France (Printed in France) 652423-03, juin 2000